Roly Bain is an itinerant full-time clown who leads and contributes to services, workshops, festivals and celebrations in churches, schools, cathedrals and all sorts of other odd places. An ordained Anglican priest, he is a founder-member of Holy Fools, a network of people for those involved in or intrigued by clown ministry. He is married to Jane, has two young children, and lives in Bristol.

Fools Rush In

A call to Christian clowning

Roly Bain

ILLUSTRATED BY
Hector McDonnell

MarshallPickering
An Imprint of HarperCollinsPublishers

For Jane, Jack and Sam
without whom . . .

Marshall Pickering is an Imprint of
HarperCollins*Religious*
Part of HarperCollins*Publishers*
77–85 Fulham Palace Road, London W6 8JB

First published in Great Britain
in 1993 by Marshall Pickering

3 5 7 9 10 8 6 4 2

Roly Bain and Hector McDonnell assert the moral right to be
identified as the author and illustrator of this work

A catalogue record for this book is
available from the British Library

ISBN 0 551 02733 9

Set in Palatino by Avocet Typesetters, Bicester, Oxon

Printed and bound in Great Britain by
HarperCollinsManufacturing Glasgow

Contents

Introduction

I was sitting in a caravan after lunch in the middle of a holiday in Salcombe in Devon. I was eight years old and I had just finished reading the autobiography of Coco the Clown – everybody's favourite clown for many years, and still a name synonymous with English clowning. On a large sheet of white paper I drew a picture of a clown in gaudy colours and costume, and fuelled by the age-old dream of running away to join a circus, I inscribed underneath ''I want to be a clown''. Many years later, quite some years after I had started clowning, my mother sent it to me, and the memory of its conception came flooding back. Clowning had been my earliest articulated ambition, and somewhere in my subconscious that clown had lurked and prodded and tickled until it had to be allowed out.

Certainly there had been other ideas. I was educated at St Paul's School, and the records show my ambitions to have been centred on playing professional football for Chelsea and England – centre forward, of course – which must have been rather galling for a rugby-playing school which prides itself on guiding its pupils towards more orthodox professions! Football gave way to catering, because I enjoyed cooking, and I began to line myself up for catering college. But then God intervened and whimsical ambition gave way to a burgeoning sense of vocation.

At first I wasn't entirely bowled over by the idea, but

in the end it happened and I never really looked back. This change of direction had all started at my school's Christian Union. I had been christened in a Methodist church – my grandfather had been a Methodist minister although he was more famous as the children's broadcaster Romany – but apart from a handful of appearances at odd Sunday Schools I had never been a churchgoer, and nor had any of the family. My grandmother had never darkened a church door since Romany's death, and that was ten years before we were born. My triplet brother Toby had started going to the Christian Union meetings a year before I did, but although a number of my friends also went I preferred to watch *The Big Match* on ITV instead. It wasn't until a football tour of Germany was called off at the last minute that I decided I'd go on one of the CU House Parties, but that was simply so that I could play lots of football with my friends. After ten days of solid football, a lot of fun, and quite a lot of "religion", I'd had the time of my life. I climbed reluctantly into the return bus in tears, and maybe it was in that tearful experience that I really found God for myself. I was fifteen and suddenly I was saying my prayers!

Two years later, at a retreat before the summer House Party, the founder of those meetings, a saint of a man called Eric Hayward, said that it might be that God was calling one of us to be ordained and that we ought not to dismiss the notion, and I felt then that he was really talking to me. The Fool always sticks his hand up and says "Here am I, send me"!

The Christian Union had a great influence on me and I continued to be involved with it for many years. It was liberal in outlook and theological bent, and it was a place where people really could enjoy themselves and be Christians at the same time. We were often unjustly proud of the accusations that we had too much fun, or that it was muscular Christianity, but the leaders took their responsibilities seriously, and our work was always seen in the context of the whole Church, with people constantly being urged to join their own local churches, to be part of other long-term worshipping communities.

The first Sunday after that first House Party, I had gone straight to what I thought was my parish church of St Mary, Barnes, but I found it rather bewildering and lonely. After the service I greeted the vicar at the door, and he promptly asked not who I was but where I lived. ''Oh, you don't belong here,'' he said ''you're supposed to go to St Michael's'', and he turned to greet the next customer. Undeterred by such a chastening experience, that was where I went.

It was the complete opposite of my Christian Union. Very high-church and extremely Anglo-Catholic, it was ruled over by Father Treadwell, who delighted in the nickname ''the Pope of Barnes'', conferred on him by no less than the then Bishop of Southwark, Mervyn Stockwood. It was there that I learned that you could laugh in church, and when I became a server, I valued the ritual and theatre of it all but soon realized that it had to be done in a sort of tongue-in-cheek way. The alternative is to take the way of doing it so seriously that you lose sight of the actual object of your devotions. Humour grants perspective, perhaps even the divine perspective, and liturgy at its best is playful – but more of that later!

I had decided to study theology at university, partly as a way of discovering and testing my vocation and partly out of interest. I reckoned that even if I didn't get ordained, at least it would be interesting and stand me in good stead. The interviewing panel at Exeter College, Oxford, decided I was trying to get in on a cheap ticket and didn't believe a word of it, so I ended up at Bristol University, where I played even more football and learned some theology in a very academic sort of way as I went along. The beauty of the Bristol Theology Department was that all the exams were pre-set, so we got the questions weeks if not months beforehand. It wasn't a recipe for hard slog and revision, for which I was grateful!

I stayed in a hall of residence for all three years in the end, and was ''in charge of'' the Monica Wills Chapel for the last two. It was there − it would have been 1973 − that I first came across, or up against, the charismatic movement which erupted in Bristol in my second year. We used to go away for weekends, and everyone else would go to the meetings and happily speak in tongues while I happily stayed in the kitchen and cooked − it was a Mary and Martha situation, but the kitchen seemed the safest place to be. I was quite content that they worshipped in their way, as long as they allowed me to worship in mine − you can only pray and worship as you can, not as you can't. I was occasionally reassured that I was top of their prayer list, for which I wasn't particularly grateful or flattered. They knew I wanted to be ordained but all they could see was a longhaired lout who was obsessed with football and who drank beer, and who, worst of all, couldn't speak in tongues. There was an awful lot of truth in their opinion of me, but it didn't stop me being a Christian − I just didn't fit their Identikit image. Being a Christian for me means being called to love and to worship

– the two great commandments. God wants me with all my strengths and weaknesses, not someone who pretends to be virtuous or terribly nice and who must fulfil a given set of criteria before being accepted into the fold. God wants me, and every other individual in the world, and he wants us now – as we are. That's part of the foolishness of God that is wiser than the wisdom of men.

There has always been a problem for me about the public image of Christians and the Church, and I know that a lot of my behaviour in the past has been geared towards overturning common perceptions of what Christians can do and what they are like. The sort of Christian who is "so heavenly-minded, he's no earthly use" is a mockery of a religion founded on the Incarnation – the story of the Ascension is a lesson in that. A clergyman is expected to be either 103 years old or a dead ringer for Derek Nimmo in *All Gas and Gaiters*. All churchgoers are assumed to be hypocrites. As a clergyman, I'm expected to approve of nothing that's remotely enjoyable! If I stick to Prayer Book services I'm an old stick-in-the-mud, but if I use modern services I'm an outrageous trendy. The list of misconceptions is endless and varied. One of my earliest missions was to flout convention and challenge the stereotypes, by embodying in myself the possibility that God wasn't choosy about who wanted to believe in him. If people could wonder "Well if he is a Christian, then I could be", maybe we'd be getting somewhere. As I later discovered, the Clown is Everyman, able to be so by the way he holds up a mirror to present us with an image of ourselves in all our foolishness. The Clown is also the great debunker and nonconformist by taste and instinct.

I left Bristol with a degree and many happy memories,

having decided that I would leap at the chance to go back there if the opportunity ever arose. I wasn't to know that fifteen years later I would return, not only as a student but a student at the circus school. As far as I knew I just wanted to be a priest. The selection process had already begun. The Diocesan Director of Ordinands, Derek Tasker, liked me, but even he admitted that he didn't think the Church would have me. He'd sent me to an Examining Chaplain who had immediately decided that my prayer life and spirituality were as shabby and scruffy as my longhaired and tousled appearance! I was sent to the Franciscans up at Llandudno for three weeks to sort out my prayer discipline, but it's still not much better than it was then . . . Anyway, Derek chose a better Examining Chaplain the second time, and eventually, much to his surprise, I sailed through the final selection conference. The selector in charge greeted me at the bottom of the stairs as I left and checked the name and directions of the pub that I worked in – the manager had written one of my references. I don't know what he wrote but it must have been good. I was sent to have a look at Westcott House and Cuddesdon Theological Colleges, plumped for Cuddesdon, and took a year off.

Cuddesdon had merged with Ripon Hall by the time I arrived. I had missed the first year of the merger but it wasn't a very happy place and there was an uneasy peace. Its nickname was Colditz – it looks dark and imposing on the skyline, it's set in what seems a remote village with no buses, and if you've no car you're stranded. But it did force me to work out properly and practically what I did believe, to make my theology my own. I hadn't had to do that in Bristol – I'd always got away with it before. But as a parish loomed closer, the time had come. And it was then that the Clown emerged.

One of the more awesome tasks at a theological college is to preach your college sermon, that is, preach to the rest of the college whom you imagine to be at their most critical, and then wait for the feedback. Having a surname like mine meant that I was second of the year on the alphabetical list. Wondering what on earth I was to preach about I hit upon the notion of the image of Jesus as Clown. On my bolder or more pious days I was to attribute that inspiration to the Holy Spirit – I can't think how else I could have come to it! And yet it all seemed to make perfect sense. I began by talking about the importance of laughter and a sense of humour, and the need to recognize and embrace the ridiculous and the absurd. I put on a red nose, asked them to imagine that they were all wearing them too, and pointed to the genuine laughter that is "the key to the Kingdom – and it is Christ the Clown prince who rules over it". I went on to portray Jesus as the Jester, the truth-teller – "a twinkle in his eye, a skip in his gait, enchanting and yet haunting, preposterous and yet he points to the truth, amusing and yet tragic. His life ends on the cross and yet he inevitably has the last laugh as he makes a mockery even of death in his resurrection." The final challenge was that they should try putting the red nose on Christ, for it would probably fit.

It was amazingly well received, and I was encouraged to write a thesis on the subject. One of the most exciting aspects was that in my research I discovered an array of kindred spirits. There was a whole movement in America devoted to "clown ministry", with thousands of groups.

To learn that there were other people on the same wacky wavelength as me was very reassuring as well as exhilarating. The thesis ended up getting top marks. It was published in shortened form in a journal called *New Life*, and I broadcast on the theme both on BBC World Service and on local radio. It informed all my thinking and all my doing. When I went as a keen young curate to St George's, Perry Hill, I wondered whether such thinking as had been conjured up in the rarefied atmosphere of Cuddesdon would stand up in "the real world". But it did.

One kindred spirit I did meet up with was Patrick Forbes, a fellow Anglican clergyman who had been to the USA on one of their week-long Clown workshops. He wanted to set one up in this country the following year, 1983, so a team was formed that included Carol Crowther of Clown Cavalcade and Sandra Pollerman, a superb storyteller, among others. It was to be the CMPDS Workshop, standing for Clown Mime Puppetry Dance and Storytelling, and we spent ages organizing it. As it happened, the Americans pulled out and as we had to pull out of the campus we had booked, but undeterred we set up a much cheaper August weekend workshop at a central London venue, to which sixty people came. We devised a whole clown service for their main Eucharist, at which I preached, and it was there that I first put on greasepaint and a huge red wig. It was a wonderful service and a privilege to be a part of it. There was a sense of being on the verge of something – it was worship on the edge of our seats. The way that the worship and the word were expressed with the chatter of puppets, the power of dance, the slapstick of clowns, the magic of story, and the gracefulness of mime combined into a heady brew that touched people's hearts. There was laughter and tears and wonder and mystery. Indeed, a bishop travelling and worshipping incognito confided afterwards that it was one of the most reverent services he had ever been to. We were up and running, and at last I was actually doing it instead of talking about it, *being* a clown rather than just being obsessed with it.

CMPDS, however, proved to be as unwieldy an animal as its title. In good clown fashion, we fell between too many stools as we tried to please too many people for too much of the time. The main organizers were all clowns, so the natural development proved to be that we renamed ourselves Holy Fools. We still offered those different disciplines but as clowns, and clowning became the focus. I have found myself performing in all sorts of places – cathedrals, schools, prisons, fêtes, churches, hospitals – anywhere where a clown might minister. At a post-Lambeth Conference celebration organized by USPG at Lichfield Cathedral we persuaded a line of twenty-two bishops to pirouette in less than graceful fashion as we encouraged the congregation to turn around and repent. One Christmas I was at Wandsworth Prison with cheering, laughing inmates, and the gift we gave them that Christmas was release from prison as they transcended the prison walls for an hour. At Guy's Hospital we gently took a group of people from a clown workshop round the children's wards and cheered and challenged and sympathized. I have no history as an actor, apart from appearing as four of the eight kings in *Macbeth* (my brother played the other four) in a school production, although public performance as a priest must help. But as a clown I continued to gain confidence and found that I could make people laugh, and as time went on I discovered that I could help them cry, too.

I ended up doing far too much of the organization of Holy Fools, and I had a rule of thumb that I shouldn't do any clowning on Sundays that interfered with my commitments to my parish. So I seemed to be doing a lot of organizing and not enough clowning myself. I'd been at Southwark Cathedral for three years and had rather more licence there because there was a large staff and I was hardly indispensable, but when I became Vicar of St Paul's, Furzedown, there was only me. We did lots of clown things there, including a series of workshops on Sunday nights and several Advent Clown Carol Services. For two years we also hosted the Annual Clowns' Service organized by Clowns International when Holy Trinity, Dalston, the Clowns' Church, was being repaired after a major fire. But when I'd been there six years I was getting restless. I knew I needed to do more clowning, to take it further, and yet I couldn't see that happening as long as I was vicar of a parish. I applied for two or three jobs that I thought might allow me to clown more, but those didn't work out. Then one night my wife, Jane, asked me what I really wanted to do. I surprised myself by saying that I really fancied going to Fool Time, the circus school in Bristol, for a year.

We must have been mad. There we were, sitting in a lovely vicarage, with two very small children asleep upstairs, contemplating leaving friends, career, and all our security behind, so that I could see if clowning was for me or not. We decided I needed to get it out of my system, if nothing else, and we knew that there was at least a possibility that I was again pursuing my vocation. I have to say that Jane has always been not just supportive but

a real part of all that I have done. When we married at
Southwark Cathedral we had clowns as ushers, and she
did quite a bit of clowning until the children arrived.
Without her I would never have done half as much as I
have. The greatest lesson I learned was the lesson of love.
I thought I knew about love and had experienced it, but
that was nothing compared to what I felt and feel about
Jane. My definition of the Clown is the vulnerable lover,
and that is not a bad description of what husband and wife
should be to each other.

Anyway, the following morning (a Thursday) I rang Fool
Time, who said I would have to come to their last audition
which was on the following Monday and Tuesday. I went,
was accepted, and the following Sunday we announced
to a startled congregation that we were off. It was the last
Sunday before the school summer holidays, and before the
end of them we had moved into Bristol, ready for the
beginning of a new life and a new term. Jane had got
herself a full-time job as a nurse, our au pair, Karyn, had
agreed to stay on for the length of the course, I eventually
managed to procure enough money from all manner of
sources to cover the fees, and both mothers stepped in at
regular intervals to bail us out.

The course was a revelation as I began to discover bits
of my body that I never even knew about and learned to
express myself physically. It was a mixture of theatre and
performance techniques and circus skills, working towards
Circus Theatre, coming from the New Circus stable.
Whereas in the past circus people had traditionally kept
the secrets of the circus to themselves and there were
distinct circus families, New Circus opens out the world
of circus skills to everyone and allows circus to be

performed in all sorts of places. Instead of having a procession of acts, and a demonstration of skills for their own sake, New Circus often tries to tell a story in the process. Rather like the Bible, the New depends on and derives from the Old and yet is a quite new departure from it, not just in content, style and approach, but also in the fact that suddenly it is seen to be for everyone rather than the chosen few.

Fool Time gave me the time and the freedom and the space to sort out my priorities as well as my clown, and it proved to be the watershed year that I had hoped. One skill that I thought I would like to learn was the slackrope, and much to my delight as well as amazement I proved to be a natural at it. Now I often perform with it as my "slackrope of faith", The course furnished me not just with the wherewithal but the confidence to carry on with my clowning in a full-time capacity and to offer myself, rather daringly, to the Church at large. What I'd wanted to discover was foolish and physical ways of presenting the Gospel, ways that I as Clown could do it, as well as simply discovering the clown that I was supposed to be. In the process I lost my huge red wig and most of my greasepainted face that had served me so well, but I knew that their time was over and that this clown was moving on. Where to, I'm not entirely sure – but that's the Fool's way.

Now I'm a full-time professional clown . . . but what is a clown? What are we actually talking about? What are the principles and the practicalities involved, the who and the why, as well as the how? This book begins as I did with the theology and theory before moving inevitably into the practice. It is meant as a manual for those who want to try Christian clowning but it is also, at least in part, meant for those intrigued by the Clown's possibilities and profoundness, and who choose to work with theory rather than practice! It offers my vision and some of my ways of working, but in the end it is up to you to make your own connections.

It all began for me with a ping-pong ball I painted red . . .

1

Red Noses Optional

NOT EVERY CLOWN HAS A RED NOSE, and not everyone who wears a red nose is a clown. The most popular image of a clown in most people's minds would be a classic circus clown with a big red nose, baggy suit, enormous shoes and extravagant make-up, with the attendant connotations of plenty of mess, water and slapstick. This is the **Auguste** clown. But he has only been around for a hundred years or so, which is only half the life of the circus itself, and there is a long parade of clowns who preceded him, each distinctive in style, attitude, role, costume and natural habitat.

Jester thrived for hundreds of years, only falling from grace with the demise of kings and their courts, for the former was his natural sparring partner, the latter his natural habitat. Colourful both in character and costume, we think of him in his traditional headwear of the "cap and bells", that rather wonky three-pronged hat with bells on. Yet that was only the refinement of centuries, and the hat itself had perhaps originated as donkey's ears to mark him out as the ass. Yet, of course, the jester was far from being an ass, for he only played the fool. Nimble both in body and mind, quick in wit and repartee, he was the insane voice of sanity in the court, the only one with the licence to tell the truth, and sometimes the only one with the vision to see it. No one and nothing was sacred as he was encouraged to transgress all boundaries, even break

23

all taboos, and as long as there was truth in his deeds and words as well as humour, he was safe. If he got it wrong he could lose his head not just his job. If he got it right then the world was his oyster and he ruled OK, till the next venture or quip. The jester was the great exponent of the art of using humour either to point to or speak of the truth, and as long as he got the balance or the chemistry right, he was rightly revered for it.

Much of the jester's comedy is based on parody and the inversion of status, for the roles of king and jester were not only interchangeable but constantly inverted. The jester, while he may have been the counterpart of the king, also complements and completes him. Each had tremendous power over the other, but of differing kinds. The one without the other loses credibility and authority – the court without its fool has neither king nor sense; but if there is no king there can be no jester and no nonsense. The top modern Russian clowns are nicknamed "Jester to His Majesty the People", which is a powerful statement in itself, but the jester and His Majesty the People cannot bounce off each other in anything like the same way. Where there is no room for nonsense, where people are allowed to take themselves far too seriously, where there is no room for humour or the ridiculous or even the imagination, then on march the despots, dictators and tyrants stage left. The jester and the kingdom endow each other with both life and meaning.

But crucial to both his success and survival was the suspicion people harboured that the Fool was somehow not of this world, and indeed that he was in touch with or perhaps even was the messenger of the gods. This is what really gave him the authority and licence to be so daringly outrageous and constantly nonconformist. The jester somehow knew things that other people couldn't know, and consequently he could also do things that other people couldn't do. The earliest jesters were usually deformed or grotesque in some way, and there is an honourable line of dwarfs and hunchbacks tailor-made for the job. The earliest known jester was a negro dwarf in the court of Pharaoh Pepi I. He could "dance the god", and the Pharaoh, in appealing to the pilot of the boat who would bring his soul to the islands of Osiris, claimed identity with his jester in the hope that it would ensure safe passage and warm welcome in the other world. In the recent film *The Black Robe*, the witchdoctor of the Indian tribe is a dwarf who carries with him the traditional jester's rod, and he is seen as the source of wisdom, the one who is in touch with the spirits; and therein lies his authority.

Ultimately the jester remains an outsider, even though he is right at the heart of things. As an outsider he can remain the detached observer of society, and pinpoint its strengths and weaknesses, as well as embody the possibility of other worlds and places.

Shakespeare's fools provide confirmation of the Fool's wisdom, if any be necessary, for it is the fools who are seen as the wise ones, it is Touchstone who is the one by whom all else are judged. The fools provide the commentary and point to the hidden agendas. Lear and his fool provide the classic king and jester situation where neither yet both are in charge, neither yet both are totally powerless, each is dependent on the other for their very existence and meaning.

Harlequin is another clown who is immediately recognizable from his diamond-patterned costume and half-mask. One of the most popular characters in the Commedia dell'Arte which began to flourish in the sixteenth century, he went on to be a star of pantomime, but once he began to lose sight of his origins and the Commedia dell'Arte connections got more and more tenuous, so he started to lose his powers and fade away. Full of mischief and fuelled by dreams, his moods swing from anger to passion to despair to happy inspiration, all at a click of the fingers. He's a lovable rogue doomed to be always frustrated. He never gets all that he needs – typically he's left starving despite his most devious wiles and extraordinary efforts to procure food for himself. He's a rather slippery customer who is none too trustworthy or reliable, but there's no doubting his intelligence, his wit or his sheer flair. Cultured and cunning he may be, but you wouldn't trust him as far as you could throw him! His only real concern is for himself.

Auguste, as we mentioned before, is the clumsy circus clown who can always be relied upon to do the wrong thing badly at the wrong time in the wrong place – and yet somehow it works! Ironically for a clown to whom all sorts of accidents happen, he was created by accident. Legend attributes it to Tom Belling who was working for Ernest Renz's Circus in Berlin in 1864. He was in the middle of a four-week suspension for falling during his act, and had been banished from the site. Feeling bored, he put his wig on back to front and his coat inside out and crept into the circus to watch the show, hoping no one would recognize him. Inevitably he came upon Renz himself, and in his confusion backed away and fell head over heels into the ring. The audience screamed with delight, assuming it all to be part of the show, and started shouting "August! August!" at him (the traditional German nickname for a clumsy idiot) and so a new clown was born and christened, all in one go.

Not all Augustes are dim-witted, some are quite clever, and yet there is a wonderful naïvety and simplicity that characterizes the Auguste that is hard to ignore. He is always the victim, the scapegoat, through no fault of his own. Playful and childlike he sweeps us along and draws us into his dreams and games, persuading us not just to follow but to accept his foolish logic. We identify with him completely because he's one of us, he's on the receiving end, he's vulnerable and he hurts. And yet whatever befalls him he picks himself up, dusts himself down and starts all over again, still with his chin up and a simple, hopeful smile on his greasepainted face.

His partner and foil is **Whiteface** who is the complete opposite of him. He wears a white conical hat rather than a battered almost unrecognizable one or a gaudy wig; his make-up, as his name suggests, is a complete white face with one or two simple and subtle lines to highlight features and distinguish him, rather than a make-up that relies on exaggeration and a contrast of bold colours to make him larger than life; a stunning, sequinned and spangled, close-fitting suit rather than a tasteless job-lot of ill-fitting garments that clash horribly with each other; shining silk stockings rather than one woolly hooped sock and one ghastly fluorescent one, both with holes in; elegant slim shoes rather than giant boots. Often musical, frequently with a selection of brass instruments, Whiteface exudes culture and class as well as a confidence born of privilege. Arrogant and pompous, he is thus essentially humourless in that he takes himself far too seriously and would be totally incapable of laughing at himself. He is happy to mock Auguste, his faithful sidekick, but is not at all happy if the tables are turned. Whiteface takes control, is always in charge, suffers the interruptions from Auguste but continues to apologize for him. Unfailingly courteous to the audience he is increasingly livid with Auguste. They are not unlike the king and jester, for their comedy as well as their tragedy is found in their unlikely partnership and the inevitable inversion of status. They might be unlikely bedfellows but they complement each other perfectly.

Tramp is even younger than Auguste. Charlie Chaplin springs jauntily to mind, with his tight buttoned jacket, baggy trousers and derby hat, twiddling and twirling that pretentious cane. Clown had found his way into the new film industry, and one of the benefits was that he could be seen to be attempting ever more impossible stunts, with the aid of celluloid and the cutting floor. He could also reach a much wider audience. Chaplin was only too aware of this and his technique was brilliant, but so was this new character. Here was the little man fighting against all the odds, a boy in a man's world. Things always happened to him that were never his fault. He leaves chaos and anarchy in his wake, but saunters on obliviously. He keeps on travelling, forever disappearing over the horizon into the sunset, hoping that tomorrow his luck will change. But it never does. He never gets the girl, he'll never be rich, he'll never get a mortgage.

One of the great discoveries that Tramp made was that you don't have to try and be desperately funny all the time, but that comedy arises from a situation or a relationship and develops if it's allowed to. Chaplin proved that if what you are doing is funny, then you don't have to be funny doing it. Just as Tramp had been born as a response to the awful depression in America when tramps and hobos abounded, and just as he had originated in the real world, so his comedy derived from it too. Perhaps that is why we identify with him so much – both he and his situation are so obviously human that it earths us and it allows us to travel with him. "There but for the grace of God go I", is a common response to the tramp's predicament, and it is Tramp who gives us the privilege and possibility of exploring what might have been.

Tramp's venture into the Circus also brought with it a breath of fresh air. Circus clowning is generally larger than life because of the sheer physical distance between the clown and the audience, especially if it's a three-ring circus. A whole troupe of clowns dash on, do something big, and charge off again in time for the next act. Tramp, however, wanders round on his own, interacting with individual members of the audience, thus introducing to the Big Top the concept of one-to-one clowning. It is rare for a smile to play across his lips, for here is the sad-sack tramp, the scruffy hobo, who has nothing to laugh about. His actions are deliberate, his manner gentle, his response usually bewildered, and his air one of great solemnity. We find him excruciatingly funny because he continues to be absolutely serious about everything he tries to do, however futile or foolish it appears to be. Everything is a problem waiting to be solved, which he achieves most improbably with a mixture of perseverance and perverse logic. Then with a characteristic shrug of the shoulders he moves on to the next problem.

Jester, Harlequin, Touchstone, Auguste, Whiteface and

Tramp provide a rich history of clowns and fools. Add to them **Trickster**, the mythological prankster and callous joker, and **Pierrot**, the melancholy romantic, and we find even more options. The image that I have of the Clown draws from all of them to greater and lesser degrees. For me the Clown is the truth-teller, the one who is licensed not just to tell but to speak of the truth. The clowns in the Commedia were the servants, especially poor old Zanni who was the lowest in the pecking order, but clowns are servants of all and often suffering servants. Like the Auguste, the Clown is the willing victim, the scapegoat and sacrifice, and yet back he comes for more, time and again, a living symbol of hope and resurrection as well as a sign of the strength of vulnerable love. He is great fun, full of jokes and laughter, and yet he is filled with a surprising sensitivity, warmth and generosity. Juggling with the paradoxes of both life and faith, he can yet carry it off and revels in that achievement. Clowns are everywhere, in all sorts of guises.

Yet the red nose remains the most powerful symbol of clowning – there is no mistaking who or what you are or what you are trying to be if there's an artificial red nose or a splodge of red greasepaint in the middle of your face. Red Noses Day in the UK has become an extremely popular way of raising money for charity, with the proceeds from any number of bizarre events going to Comic Relief. All sorts of people, especially public luminaries, are persuaded to wear a red nose for the day, and the more important or improbable the wearer, the better. It allows people to make absolute fools of themselves in a good cause, and it also allows people to use their imaginations to dream up the most absurd and novel antics that might persuade others to part with money. It's all great fun, but it's all much of a muchness. It's a day for Augustes. Once again the public perception of a clown is reduced to the Auguste's basic limits, and we don't take the red nose further than the office joker. Red Nose Day has probably unearthed lots of wonderful clowns, or at least unlocked a vast potential. The beautiful thing to do would be to take it further, to help them enter into the mystery that is their own clown inside them, to help them see further than the end of their red noses to what lies at the heart of it all. When we begin to discover all of that, then the red nose becomes an even more powerful symbol, and we also find that we can dispense with it as part of our costume if we so desire. It provides a way in but we don't need to hang on to it if it ends up being inappropriate.

What a number of clowns in recent years have discovered is that clowns don't need a uniform – say a broad-checked suit and big boots, nor even much greasepaint – and there's a whole generation of ''naturalistic'' clowns with clothes that are only slightly exaggerated versions of ordinary wear and a minimal amount of make-up. There seem to be more character clowns around too – my own clown remains a vicar! This is a natural progression from Tramp, where the real world is being reflected in clowning. This must be a good thing because that is where the clowns should be – bang slap up in the real world. Clowns who are not larger-than-life challenge us even more because they more accurately reflect our own foolishness. Part of the clown's role and task is to hold up a mirror to everyone so that they can see themselves in him, and while we may be able to write a clown off if he is too fantastic or overblown, it's more difficult if he somehow looks rather like us or the person next door.

It's much more scary to be a clown without the aid of lashings of make-up, an immediately recognizable outlandish costume and a favourite prop, but it works for some people. I'm not saying that this is what everyone should aim at, as if this is the best way – it's just one way of clowning to put alongside the other options. Whether you're going to be a naturalistic clown or an Auguste, you still have to discover the clown that is within you and let it live. It may be that a tramp character is appropriate, but it may be that you just want to be you or that you don't fit into a type. It means that you are not only left to your own devices but that you are entirely dependent on your own resources. That leaves you feeling very vulnerable, but it is exactly that vulnerability which is the clown's major resource. That's where you start from. It is the clown's vulnerability that makes him so accessible and lovable and open, and yet it is that same vulnerability that is so challenging to a society of people who pursue impregnability and robust health and who lock themselves away in mortgaged houses to count their life insurance.

There's no such thing as the definition of a clown – we've already seen how many types and sorts there are. People have tried, of course, but it's a really foolish thing to do! Clowns defy everything, especially definition. Yet my favourite description of a clown is one coined by Colin Morris in a book called *Hammer of the Lord* and that is "the vulnerable lover". If you're vulnerable you can allow things to happen and you're never quite in charge of any situation. There is a sense in which you're seeing everything for the first time, everything is new because you carry no history with you, no tried and trusted ways of behaviour and evasion. You put yourself in vulnerable situations because you always take risks and you always say "Yes!" "Yes, of course I'll jump off that cliff. Yes, of course I'll go and visit that smelly old lady. Yes, of course I'll make friends with the class bully." It's in taking risks that we discover not just our vulnerability but also the extent of our own resources. The jester lived by his wits and resourcefulness, and every clown has to do the same. Being vulnerable then involves allowing things to happen but it also demands that we make things happen – we don't know what things, but that's where the risk lies. Clowns challenge the status quo, they question, they turn things upside down and inside out. Nothing is safe, just as nothing is sacred. Anarchy is inevitable when our ordered existence is thrown into disarray.

But all of that can be done in the gentlest way because the clown is the vulnerable lover, and love informs and is the basis of all that he does. We love the clown partly because he is who he is. We are able to love him because he loves us – the relationship is a two-way one, as it must be. We also love him because he is able to love himself. The vulnerable lover accepts all his imperfections and weaknesses, acknowledges his own absurdity, has discovered and has access to all his emotions, explores his dreams, lives his hopes, knows his strengths, and gets on with it. In loving the clown we are able to love ourselves too, for again it is our own self that we see reflected in him.

A golden rule of clowning is that the clown, like love, must always allow the other person space. Everyone has their own private space around them wherever they are, and you can tell its boundaries as you begin to approach them. If it's obvious that you are encroaching, then you have to back off; but if it's apparent that they welcome you in, then you're in business. It really isn't acceptable to ignore the initial responses that an adult or a child may make, nor just to ride roughshod over their feelings. There are plenty of adults today who will tell of awful experiences with clowns in their childhood. It can be funny to squirt a child with water or smother an adult in custard pies, but only if they are willing victims, only if they want to play. To make someone suffer isn't much fun for anyone, least of all the victim. So love allows space and often therefore time, and there is an invitation to play. The clown shouldn't force himself on anyone. Love invites, love is playful, love delights in the beloved. A lot of clowning is simply playing games, inventing games, taking things to absurd ends and yet logical conclusions.

Love can bring everything to a standstill. It certainly upsets the best-laid of plans. It turns everything topsy-turvy. It sends us off on tangents. It daydreams and desires. Love sets the pulse racing. Love is full of expectancy, it leaves us on the edge of our seats. It's exciting and worrying and demanding and exhilarating. We're never quite the same once love has struck.

Love has commitment to the other person which will not allow unnecessary pain or grief, and which will do anything for the beloved. The clown cares about the other, stands up for the other, wants the best for the other. There are no cheap jokes at the other's expense, only at one's own cost. The clown's love is a love that is faithful and true and does not count the cost. Love is truthful and has no secrets. It both delights in the truth and is prepared to be open. Being truthful enables the clown to perceive truth when he sees it.

Love is passionate and emotional. Clowns who might as well be plastic or cardboard cut-outs are no use to anyone. Part of being vulnerable is allowing our emotions in to play and following them through. Tears are the clown's trademark, but it isn't just tears of sorrow, it's also tears of laughter. Clowns allow themselves to reach the heights and the depths because that way it's much more risky, but also it's the way to live life to its fullest, to live it up to the brim. Once we're familiar with our emotions then we can begin to play with them and to live that full life. Emotions move us on as well as move us. They are part of our resources, but they are also part of ourselves and nothing to be frightened of. People who are emotional are often written off as being foolish, and people in tears apologize for making a fool of themselves, but why apologize for being foolish?

Being a clown is wonderfully liberating for it allows our own self out to play, and we find that actually he isn't nearly as awful or dull or outrageous or whatever as we feared. Being a clown liberates ourselves to be ourselves, and that is ultimately why the clown is beyond definition. Every true clown is an individual and quite unique. Whatever his garb or motley or type, within that framework he is inimitable, There is an old tradition that Clowns International have resurrected, which is that each clown's make-up is copied on to an egg and that acts as a kind of copyright. Just as no one can use your name, so no one can use your make-up. That's a fair testament to the uniqueness of each of us. A clown's make-up depends on the shape and contours of his face, on his emotions and moods, as well as on clown type, and no one is exactly the same as another. Paradoxical as ever, the Clown is Everyman, and yet there is no one quite like him; he is his own man and yet belongs to everyone. The Clown is you and me, and is in you and me. Help!

2

The Foolishness of God

TO SAY THAT THE CLOWN is in me and in you is a statement about the God in whose image we are made. God has given us the possibility and the capability of dealing with our fallibility, not by feeling terribly guilty about it but by accepting it and laughing about it and transforming it. God could have created a race of sparklingly infallible Whitefaces who would have sent serpents and interlopers packing, but he chose to create humans with the capacity for love and laughter, tears and temptations. The Fall was inevitable. But then pratfalls are when clowns are on stage. Was that so terribly foolish of God?

To see God as our Creator is to see the God who revels in his own creativity as well as all that he creates, who enjoys the broad strokes as well as the tiny details that make up the complexities of creation. God is the God who is Love, and his love shines through all that he creates. His love is the love that is laughter, a liberating love with a redeeming smile that is a way of transcendence and salvation. The love that is laughter is a gurgling, rumbling, irrepressible love that wells up from the very depths, is quite uncontrollable, irresistible, seems to split us in two. It makes us helpless, and leaves us changed and full of hope, having glimpsed something of another world, if not the eternal.

God's greatest creation remains us, and to us he gives

the great gift of a sense of humour. A sense of humour gives us perspective. Nothing is ever as bad or as good as it seems, and nor is any person as good or as bad as they seem. Everybody has a sense of humour because it's part of the package that God gives us. Maybe sometimes it seems to be driven out of or suppressed in people, but no one who has once laughed is beyond hope. Even in the most evil of people there is that one chink of light, that little ray of laughter that tells us all is not lost. Myriad are the tales of humour in the most awful of situations. Perhaps the most striking is the sense of humour displayed by the Jews in the concentration camps. If humour can still surface, never mind flourish, in such situations, then surely there is a sign of the presence of God. Humour brings hope and all sorts of possibilities. Humour lets us look at things differently, from a different angle. It grants us the divine perspective.

Humour stops us being weighed down by matters of consequence and very important people because we suddenly realize that it isn't a matter of life and death that this gets finished by Friday, and that the bank manager doesn't actually bite. Humour reminds us of the real world and pulls us out of the cul-de-sacs we keep getting stuck in. It reminds us that all people are equal and that all things are possible and that some things can wait. Humour puts a rose in the boss's teeth and a leotard on the charlady and asks us to take them seriously. Humour tests priority, pomposity and pretentiousness. It is a solid gauge of authenticity, removing our blinkers and pointing to the truth.

Humour helps us out of the dull world of predictability, providing surprising denouements and alternative endings to tickle our fancy and foster our imaginations. It teaches us to live for the moment in case we miss that moment which could be the highlight of the day, that moment of incongruity which lifts us out of our imprisonment and sheds new light on old and familiar ways and people. Humour digs us out of the rut as well as the pit. One of the great privileges of clowning in prisons is that it offers an escape route for prisoners that goes far beyond the prison walls. In their laughter they fly up and away, and for an hour at least life is good.

Humour differs from person to person and culture to culture, of course, but it doesn't always matter that somebody else doesn't get the joke just as long as we do. Communicating the joke is a different skill! Humour can be vicious and sick and we can use it for our own ends, but that's a travesty of God's gift. True humour is inseparable from love, and it is loveless humour that perverts truth, distorts our vision of the world and of God, and stunts the growth of our imagination, dulling our senses and sensitivity. When humour feeds on love, then truth is revealed, our vision of the world and of God is clarified, our imagination runs riot, our senses are heightened and our sensitivity increased.

Laughter can be abused too. It can be exclusive or cruel or demeaning or mocking. It can be shallow or hollow or artificial or forced. It can be a safety net when all else fails, a safety curtain to keep others at a distance, or a safety valve that simply reduces the stress and the pressure. It can be used as a weapon of self-preservation and deception. Laughter can be stifled and all but eradicated by dictators, famines, hardship and plagues, but it always returns like a guardian angel, assuring us that God has his foot in the door. Genuine laughter is the laughter of love, true love is the love that is laughter, and true humour is inseparable from love. That is the heady brew that God offers us.

The Garden of Eden was a playground for mankind to play in. There was only one rule of the game and of course it got broken. Adam began to take himself very seriously indeed, but when he bit the apple he suddenly got the joke and saw that there was no way that man could be like God, though it wasn't going to stop him working at it. God played hide-and-seek with Adam for a while, but God knew where he was hiding all the time, and knew what he'd done – fathers always do. When God took his turn to hide, Adam got distracted by his work and never got round to looking until it was too late. He's been looking for that playground ever since. It never occurred to him that it might be inside him.

The God that man can play with is also the God he can share a joke with, complain to, chat to, or simply burst into tears with. When God told Abraham and Sarah that they were going to have a baby they assumed he was joking. But this time he wasn't. Nevertheless, they called their son Isaac, the laughing one or laughter, because of it. It's interesting to note that Abraham was prepared even to sacrifice laughter in order to keep his God happy, but God knew how important it was, not just for the future of Israel, and stopped him. The only laughter of God that we find in the Old Testament is the laughter of mockery and scorn as God is seen either to relish defeating all Israel's enemies or to get one back on the Israelites themselves after one of their regular bouts of unfaithfulness.

But the laughter of mockery and scorn, as well as being

a mockery of true laughter, is the laughter of the in-crowd, and the God of the Old Testament was seen as the God of the in-crowd. It wasn't until the joke was shared that it could become universal. It wasn't until Jesus that God was seen to be the God of everybody. The most foolish thing of all about God was that he was prepared to come and do something about it so that everybody could get the joke, everybody could join in the laughter of God. Suddenly they realized that the laughter of God was always of pleasure and delight rather than the opposite. And Jesus didn't come as an all-conquering military hero or a comic-book superhero – that really would have been a joke. He came in the normal way, born of a woman. How wonderfully foolish for God to be born, not even as a man but as a baby. How wonderfully foolish to be born at all. Here was God in all his foolish vulnerability at the mercy of the world and the people he loved. And the wise and the simple came to witness the birth of the vulnerable lover. How they laughed and rejoiced.

As at the beginning, so at the end Jesus in all his foolish vulnerability hung on the cross at the mercy of the world and the people he loved. And the wise and the simple came to witness the death of the vulnerable lover. How they laughed and mocked. Yet they ought to have known that the clown is irrepressible – you just can't kill him off. He always returns, maybe in another guise in a different place from where you expect him, but he's back, and even more the clown than he was before. And three days later Jesus was back in a selection of guises in the places you least expected him. He had had the last laugh on death itself and the empty tomb echoed with the sound of God's laughter. Isaac was spared the sacrifice, Jesus wasn't. But there is no comedy of resurrection without the tragedy of crucifixion. The sickest joke of which man could conceive was God's crucifixion, but nobody found it very funny. It was God who provided the most glorious and surprising punchline of all, saving the best joke till last in order to transform man's worst into God's best. Comedy and tragedy are thinly divided – two sides of the same coin. A flip of the coin made all the difference. Three days later, when the coin landed, life would never be the same again, for Jesus was back, full of the love that is laughter.

But let's not turn Jesus into Harlequin, a slippery customer who cheats death and then dines out on the story for the rest of his life. It would be just like Harlequin to fake his death in order to guarantee filling his stomach. Harlequin's schemes never quite work anyway – they only work in his dreams. Crucifixion ensured there was no faking Jesus' death and no avoiding the agony of dying. Jesus didn't "do a Lazarus" by rising from the dead only to die of old age at a later date – a strange fate that would have been, as well as a terrible anti-climax. He finished in good pantomime style, disappearing through a trapdoor in the clouds to fulfil the expectations of the audience, only to reappear moments later back down below, tapping one of them on the shoulder. All that's missing is the crowd's cry of "He's behind you!" He hadn't gone at all – the promise was to be with us always, to the end of time, and he keeps reappearing with a tap on the shoulder to remind us.

But Jesus is only capable of such low comedy because he was prepared to suffer the agonies of high tragedy. There is no evidence in the Bible of Jesus laughing at all, but that may be because it was taken for granted. There is evidence of him in tears. There are tears of compassion at the grief of Mary and Martha over the death of Lazarus, and tears of frustration over the intransigence of Jerusalem. It is pure conjecture but it seems unlikely that there were not tears of laughter too from the man accused of being a drunkard and a friend of sinners, who held court at dinner parties with such memorable stories, who had a boundless store of punchlines for his parables, and who revelled in the abundant life and the love that is laughter. Jesus the vulnerable lover is recognizable as Christ the Clown, and in both images we discover the God of Tears.

For the Christian God is the God who cries with us and laughs with us, sharing our sorrows and joys and frustrations, and who cries for us when there are no tears there and laughs for us when it's the last thing we feel like doing. God is found in tears, for it is when we are in tears that we are at our most vulnerable, our defences are down, and God gets a peep over the parapet. He won't gatecrash because that's not his way; he'll wait to be invited in. But whether invited or not, he's there in our tears. He's there in our tears because he loves us. When tears are shared there is real communion because there is total love and trust. People who love each other cry together in the good times as well as the bad, because to cry alone with sorrow or frustration is awful and to cry alone with joy is selfish. Crying together is the way of growth. And God knows our loneliness and our grief as well as our causes for rejoicing, because he's experienced those feelings and occasions himself in the person of Jesus and he can enter into our experience in our tears.

The Clown is the suffering servant of the people. There is a mythology about clowns that they are all desperately unhappy people in private. Generally it's not true, though it does testify to the ability of the Clown to reach both the heights and the depths. The Clown knows that the price for reaching the heights is the ability to fall to the depths, but he also knows it's worth it. Like Jester, the Clown is at the whim of his master and he knows that the show must go on, whatever his personal and private problems and agonies. If he doesn't get it right he'll be punished, even executed. His task is to satisfy all the needs of all the people all the time, and because he knows that nothing is impossible he attempts it every time, with every confidence that this time he'll get it right. And sometimes he gets it horribly wrong, sometimes he dies a death, figuratively or actually. But he keeps returning from the dead, rising again to scale new heights and chart new depths. He is at the beck and call of everyone, man, woman or child, for as long as he is dressed in motley he must do all that is asked of him, and more. If a child wants a trick, you do a trick, assuming you can. If a man wants a miracle, you perform a miracle, assuming you can and it's appropriate. Love suffers and serves but it can also transform. It goes through hell and high water to do what is asked of it. The foolishness of God is not only that he'll do anything for anyone but that in the person of Jesus he has already done it – for everyone.

But whatever the cost the Jester's principal aim is to point to and speak of the truth. In Jesus we see the embodiment of the truth-teller. Truth may speak for itself but it cannot really be proclaimed or spelt out; it may be hinted at, conveyed and whispered, but it cannot be rammed down people's throats; truth has somehow to become intimate and personal before it can be taken on board. Jesus wasn't the first to discover that humour is an ideal method of conveying the truth. Truth is blindingly obvious once you've recognized it, once you've got the joke. In that moment of getting the joke, its truth becomes your truth and you own it for yourself. When Jesus proclaimed himself as the Way, the Truth and the Life (John 14), it seemed that there was Truth for the taking, but poor old Philip didn't get the joke, he couldn't take it in, and once again Jesus had to start explaining what he meant as well as what he stood for. Jesus was often accused of speaking in riddles, but riddles are one of the Jester's favourite pastimes. Riddles test and tease. You need to enter into them, be on the right wavelength, even be in the right mood to solve the most difficult ones. But all riddles have an answer and those who are committed to seeking the answer will find it. Riddles that appear absolutely non-sensical are suddenly discovered to make perfect sense, to contain the truth. Truth, like the Jester's very garb, rings bells. When bells ring, as all schoolchildren know, we should rejoice that another lesson has been learned and we can move on.

In the search for truth, one lesson that has to be learned quickly is the art of asking the right questions – you can't get the right answers if you're not asking the right questions. The next lesson is simply to ask the right questions regardless of whether they have answers or not. It's all part of the knack of pointing to truth. The Clown is himself a big question mark, querying all that goes on, challenging all whom he meets. The Clown always asks "Why?" Nothing and no one is taken for granted, nothing and no one is taken as read. So Jesus looked at the religion of his time and at the religious leaders and began to ask questions. He looked at the society in which he lived and began to ask questions. He looked at the people who surrounded him and asked more questions. He looked in his own heart and his own life and began to ask more questions still. Why? and Who? and Where? and When? are the real questions. How doesn't really matter! It can't matter when the Clown knows that nothing is impossible because there is always a way. Jesus knew that with God nothing was impossible, and what he began to discover was that he himself was actually the way. That was pretty frightening, but being a question mark is not a safe thing to be. Being a question mark causes revolution because the Clown turns everything upside down and inside out in his attempts to sort things out – and often when things are inverted we discover they were upside down and inside out all along. Jesus the Clown proclaimed the first last and the last first, and that you had to lose your life to find it. People were to be like the humble if sinful publican, not the self-righteous Pharisee who played it by the book. Women and children were just as important as men because all were equal in the eyes of God. Enemies were to be loved, commitment was to be total, and Caesar was to be obeyed as long as God was too.

Jesus picked ears of corn on the sabbath, paid his taxes from the mouth of a fish, missed the boat so walked across the water to catch up with it, upset the tables of the money-lenders, and entered Jerusalem not on a mighty charger but on a humble ass. Whatever he did and said asked questions of his audience. When he cast demons out of Legion and into the Gadarene swine they jumped off the cliff like lemmings, proving once and for all that pigs can't fly. Some suspected him to be the devil himself, and that he cast out devils by Beelzebub the Prince of Devils. Part of the clown's mystique is that people are never quite sure if he is diabolical or divine in origin, whether to polish his halo or shine his cloven hoof. When Jesus came walking across the water to his disciples they thought first of all that he must be a ghost, an emissary from the underworld, until he got closer. The wonderful story of the temptation in the wilderness has Jesus being tempted to try cheap tricks and outrageous stunts, like turning stone into bread or throwing himself off the precipice so that a whole legion of angels could catch him in a safety net. But here was the Clown playing the part of the Lord of Misrule, the Lord of Disorder, causing chaos and anarchy in pursuit of order so that when all the pieces of the puzzle were put back together again they would form a very different picture of God.

Who but a clown would want to move mountains or calm the raging seas? Who but a clown could envisage camels wriggling through eyes of needles and wolves prancing around in sheep's clothing? Who but a clown could get away with all he said about the scribes and Pharisees? Who but a clown could juggle so adroitly with the paradoxes of his faith and life, keeping comedy and tragedy, humanity and divinity, life and death, the demands of his God and his religion in tension?

Here was Jesus the Clown, vulnerable and gentle, passionate and powerful. Brimful with love and laughter, wit and wisdom, his was the clown's transforming touch in a world of miracle and mystery, where people could be made whole by deed or word, water could become vintage wine, and bread and wine become his body and blood. Full of compassion and courage, here was the God of Tears incarnate, a capering, cajoling, challenging Christ imbued with a deep peace and a divine restlessness. His disciples were to be like him, especially after he'd gone. He would still be there with them, even to the end of time, but he was going to send another helper. This was to be no stooge, but the Holy Spirit who would breathe not just life but laughter into Christ's Church: the laughter of fellowship and heartfelt joy, of hope and truth, of faith and triumph. If God is to be found in our tears, then the Holy Spirit is found above all in our tears of laughter.

3

The Clown's Church

PERHAPS ONE OF THE MOST surprising and encouraging things about the Church is that it is built on a pun. The first disciples are simple fishermen, presumably quite happy in their work and their lives. Jesus comes along and challenges them to be fishers of men rather than fish. Instead of packing him off with a curse and a retort such as "You must be joking", which would be quite justifiable in the circumstances, the opposite occurs. Simon and Andrew get the joke, drop everything, and follow him.

Simon soon gets the nickname of Peter the Rock, because Jesus chooses him as the rock on which the Church will be built, and yet Rocky would have been a better name, for the rock doesn't settle for a long, long time. Rocky is the eternal first volunteer, the one who steps forward first without thinking about it, the one who sets off to walk upon the water to meet Jesus but then realizes where he is and sinks beneath the waves. Rocky is a rough and ready bodyguard committed to protecting his master, but the moment he glows with pride at being given the responsibility of being the Rock, the very next moment he is dashed by the burning shame of being cast as the villain of the piece, not a rock but a stumbling block. Rocky hasn't really got a clue about what's going on. Up on the Mount of Transfiguration he wants to build three shelters so that Moses and Elijah and Jesus can stay there, or perhaps return there, as if there's a need either for a new branch of the office or three holiday chalets. When Jesus washes his disciples' feet Rocky can't handle it and protests. Even when he concedes, he still asks for his hands and head to be washed too. For Rocky it's all or nothing. Rocky, the holy henchman, is full of bluster and good intentions. He wants to do something to help Jesus after he is arrested, but all that happens is that he denies him three times, and it takes the cock's crow to bring him finally to his senses. John's gospel provides us with the counterbalance of the three denials as Peter, still puzzled but faithful, protests three times to Jesus, "You know that I love you".

Here stands the vulnerable lover, the holy fool, the improbable Peter. The clown always says "yes", and thinks about it afterwards. He takes huge risks partly because that is the stuff and the adventure of life, and partly because they don't seem like huge risks to him even if they do to others. Committed to living each moment of the day as if it were his last, he is a collector of moments. There are some he would dearly love to stick into his scrapbook but ultimately he knows it's a hopeless task. Yet the clown represents the triumph of hope over experience. He keeps picking himself up, dusting himself down and starting all over again. It doesn't matter how many times he gets it wrong or puts his great big foot in it, because there's always another chance. The clown has his own logic and pursues it – it's quite simple and obvious to him, however tortuous it may look from the outside – and he gets there in the end. Peter is the Auguste in the troupe of apostles. Maybe there were others too but we know very little about most of them. Peter is the butt, the victim of the jokes who keeps coming back for more. He is the one who gets all our sympathy, carries our hopes, and finally triumphs despite and because of all that has gone on before.

Peter is transformed in the experience of Pentecost and the coming of the Holy Spirit. The Twelve are filled with the Holy Spirit, and in the ensuing joyful delirium they begin to babble in many tongues. They are accused of being drunk, but Peter rises to the occasion. He is the first to realize what is happening. He doesn't get on his high horse and start protesting that this is a deeply religious experience, his first riposte is simply to say that they can't be drunk yet because it's too early in the day – irrefutable logic and a lovely putdown of the hecklers. Then he goes on to preach as he has never done before and three thousand souls are baptized.

It's not that he's not foolish any more, it's just that suddenly he's got the words because everything's fallen into place and his faith is finally founded on rock, just as the Church soon would be. The missing piece in this particular puzzle was the Holy Spirit, and without it there wasn't a hope. Peter still took enormous risks, remained as impulsive as ever, blustered to the end, and as always it was all or nothing. He remained vulnerable and humble and loving. It was said that if even his shadow passed over a sick person that person was healed, and somehow that's typical of Peter who never really knew what was happening from one moment to the next, was often totally oblivious of his effect on other people, and retained a simple naïvety and lack of pretension till the day he died. He followed his master's fate in being crucified in the end, but even then he was turned topsy-turvy and crucified upside down. Perhaps that was in recognition of the fact that he and the Holy Spirit had turned the world upside down, and this was punishment in kind.

Peter is a model not just for popes but for the whole Church, for all who would call themselves Christians. That is not to say that we have to follow his example in specifics, because Peter's foolishness expressed itself in one way while ours may manifest itself in others. But if Peter is still standing at the pearly gates waiting to have a set of keys delivered to him, he'll want to have a word with, if not stop, anyone who has taken themselves too seriously. After all, it is in the nature of the Auguste to give a Whiteface a hard time!

It's quite a thought, to be teased at the gates of heaven, but it's quite possible. To look back on our lives, especially from the viewpoint and in the context of heaven, would surely make us laugh, with delight at some bits but also with disbelief at some of our errors and feeble attempts and frequent self-deceptions and pretensions. We are quite laughable, if we would but admit it. Looking back might make us cry too, not with regret but with genuine sorrow, and those tears of sorrow mixed with tears of laughter would lead us to a real repentance and maybe even a sudden appreciation of our true selves if not the actual self-realization. But the greatest joke of all for Peter is the smile on the face of all those who have made the greatest efforts and most earnest attempts to get into heaven, for they don't realize yet that everybody else gets in too. Many are the jokes based on there being great walled areas in heaven within which live those who think they are the only ones there. Yet everybody's invited, all are on the guest list, nobody is refused entry. The foolishness of God is that he loves everyone and forgives everyone and that his grace is limitless. This vulnerable God can hang on the cross or hide behind the gatepost of heaven and be rejected by the people he loves – that's their prerogative – but he isn't going to follow their example.

"Ah, but," objects the Whiteface, "what's the point of going to church?" "What's the point of being a Christian?", replies the Fool. There's such a difference between faith and religion. It's an over-simplification, but the Fool has faith while the Whiteface makes do with religion. The Fool has faith and knows it because it is an affair of the heart. He never quite knows what to do with it, apart from maybe express it in worship and share it with other people. If he finds it wonderful he's bound to tell other people about it. The Fool naturally desires to love God and other people. The Whiteface makes do with religion because that's a safer bet, a safer place to be. He knows exactly what he's got to do, how and when he's got to do it, and where. He may not know why, but that doesn't trouble him too much. He may have had faith once but it's been superseded. He doesn't have to ask questions any more, he just gets on with it the way he's been shown. Making do with religion is dangerous because it begins to be secondhand rather than first, depends on the man-made rather than divine inspiration, goes through the motions rather than allowing him to be moved by the Spirit, lives in the future rather than the present.

The Church is full of Whitefaces, of course, for whom any accusations of hypocrisy, airs and graces or simply social convention fall on deaf ears. Whitefaces like to be in charge and be seen to be in charge, taking themselves and their role terribly seriously. Unable to suffer fools gladly, they are often patronizing in the extreme. Busy and bossy, they always know best in the nicest possible way. They are more likely to collect committees than moments!

Whitefaces talk about it while Fools get on with it and go for it. It is easy to write off the Church as Whiteface: haughty, bejewelled, more concerned with itself than with others, and thus with no real clue about the real world. But the Church isn't like that in most places, even if those churches with hierarchies might lead us to believe it is. And anyway, there is a sense in which the Church needs its Whitefaces as much as anyone else. It's when there is a preponderance of them that there is a problem. Whitefaces like to take centre stage and they tend to take the eye, so it is hardly surprising that the Church ends up with a Whiteface reputation. But where there are Whitefaces there are also bound to be Augustes.

A Church that contained only Augustes would be even more disastrous than a Church containing only Whitefaces. The Auguste's Church is tempting in some ways. It would be a Church that was happy to take risks, that lived for the moment, that always got there in the end thanks to its own peculiar logic. But it would be a Church that never got very far, that had no direction or organization, that never learned from its mistakes. It would be bright and big and colourful and larger than life, with voluminous pockets to fit everything in. But it would be forever falling over its enormous feet, would seem to have no control over its limbs and organs, and might just be too loud too often. But however great the Auguste's bravado and however brazen his appearance, it is the underlying vulnerability that is at once so tempting and so obvious. The Auguste is always a victim, always gets teased or beaten up and bullied. The Auguste is always on the receiving end. How different it would be to be part of a Church that was always wiping custard pies off its face! There's usually one custard pie because the Auguste never quite ducks in time, and there's often a second because he turns the other cheek – as he is bound to. Gullible to an all but implausible degree, the Auguste's naïvety is akin to the childlikeness that is enjoined upon all Christians, and it is his childish vulnerability that is so appealing and yet makes us fear for him so. Playful and plucky he keeps bouncing back for more, whatever befalls him, but his resilience cannot hide the hurt he feels. The Auguste's Church would be full of Christians with genuine smiles on their faces, prepared to be hurt for the sake of others, whose love was sacrificial and who were always at the service of others, prey to their every whim and fancy. Their faith would be simple, their needs basic, and there wouldn't be a synod in sight!

Maybe the Church as Tramp has something to offer us too. There's a restlessness about the Tramp in the way he keeps moving on that speaks of the pilgrim Church. He has nowhere to rest his head, no place to call home, and yet everywhere is his home. He has no possessions apart from what he carries and wears, and yet the world is his and everything belongs to him. He seems to have no control over his destiny, or has long since renounced control by choice or lost it through circumstance. The Church as Tramp is the Church of the oppressed and the marginalized. Tramp is the unwelcome reminder of our own good fortune. He represents a challenge to our sense of security and comfort, our standard of living, even our values and morality. Unhurried and unashamed, he wanders and begs and muses, happy to accept hospitality and charity, to share what he's been given, and to move on once more, leaving no ties or burdens, debts or grudges behind him. The Tramp is in the world and yet somehow not of it. He has neither the time nor the taste for glory, pomp and circumstance. Dependent on others for sustenance he yet chooses to remain alone and keep his own company. Miserable as he looks, we suspect he's happy and contented. Scornful of an even keel, there are great depths which he has dared to plumb and mighty heights he has scaled. He is the great outsider who can never be on the inside, the nonconformist for whom nothing is certain or sacred. But looking in from the outside gives him the perspective that others miss out on and those deceptively bleary eyes are watchful and miss nothing. The Tramp sees all and sees through all. And yet if Whiteface greets us with a scowl, and Auguste with a smile, Tramp greets us with a frown. There is no real warmth or welcome until a trust can be established, and the Tramp's Church is not designed for those who need to know exactly where they are and why, nor for those who need to feel wanted or valued, even loved.

But whichever clown we took as a model it wouldn't be sufficient or complete because there are elements of all of them that would be necessary and desirable in the Clown's Church. One thing the Clown's Church wouldn't do would be to take itself seriously. What the medieval Church did to counteract any excess of gravity was to stage an annual Feast of Fools. These happened throughout Europe and were held right at the beginning of the New Year, probably coinciding with the old Feast of the Circumcision (a suitably ludicrous feastday!). It was a day for topsy-turvydom and anarchy as the lower ranks of the clergy and the people went on the rampage. Priests wore bawdy masks at services and out in the streets, people danced and jumped and somersaulted in church and sang outrageous songs, the minor clerics donned the robes of their superiors and paraded their new exalted status, and dice and all sorts of games were played in the sanctuary. The solemn rituals of both Church and Court were parodied: the thurible of incense was replaced with a pair of old smoking boots, and while the priest said mass the people ate cake, black puddings and sausages at the altar. In some places a boy bishop was elected and he presided over a mock mass and received obeisance due to such a dignitary. Elsewhere a beautiful girl was led up to the sanctuary on an ass and the Kyrie Eleison (Lord, have mercy) was sung as three hee-haws; at the end of the mass the dismissal took the form of three more hee-haws, with the response the same.

Whatever form it took nobody and nothing was exempt from the treatment. The festivities would often begin with, and certainly revolve around, the verse from the Magnificat, "he has put down the mighty from their seats and has exalted the humble and meek". Although there was an obvious and complete inversion of role and status as the whole Church was made a huge mockery of, it was only fun and valid because those who participated in the revels actually attached great importance to the Church and their worshipping lives. The antics of the Feast of Fools provided a perspective that put things in their proper place. The Church was not so sacrosanct and our religious lives not as set apart then as they appear to be now. It seems to be true that we joke most about those things that we hold most dear, and can be teased most about those things and people whom we love and to which we are committed. The Feast of Fools provided that healthy and humorous outlet for the Church for several centuries, but it was inevitably unpopular with some of the powers-that-be. As early as 1199 the Feast was forbidden by the Bishop of Paris, but despite the efforts of reformers and ecclesiastics and the outright denunciation by the Council of Basel in 1431, it didn't finally die out until the end of the sixteenth century. The Reformation firmly shut the lid on any attempts at this style of celebration and festivity. In England, for instance, the Puritans set out with great reforming zeal to eradicate all traces of medieval catholicism, which meant that the colour and the theatre and the art and the festivals went with it. Gradually the Protestant work ethic predominated as work was seen to be the way to holiness and salvation, while the virtues of thrift, sobriety, diligence and moderation were commended. Leisure and play were dismissed as being of little value, and if not a necessary evil then an irritating necessity. Festivity and fun were no longer seen as valid ways of communing with God, laughter was banished from the churches, and the Church had to be taken very seriously indeed.

Yet the Church must be able to laugh at itself and allow itself to be laughed at. If we forbid it or avoid it, it suggests a faith that is too fragile, a Church that is built on sand rather than rock. A Church built on rock is grateful for gales of laughter and the waves of wit and parody, not because it is proofed against them but because that is exactly the place where it should be. It is good to be washed over with humour, to be teased off high horses and out of self-importance. Holiness without humour can be less than human and far from divine.

There is a long and honourable tradition of holy fools in the Church, especially in the Orthodox Churches. My favourite is St Francis of Assisi, whose followers were called *joculatores* or merrymakers, and it was said that the highways and byways resounded with laughter when he and his were around. But often the holy fools were so called not because of their humour but because of their humiliation. Harrowed by the humiliation that Jesus suffered on the way to and on the cross, many took it upon themselves to follow that example and hoped to be humiliated as much as was humanly possible. Therefore many roamed the country naked, feigned madness, begged for all their food, and raved and ranted and preached in their own peculiar ways. They delighted in mockery and degradation. Yet they evoked awe and wonder and many were canonized. Peter Barnes in his play *Red Noses* offers us a wonderful image of people of this ilk, with the group of Flagellants who keep appearing on stage whipping themselves or bashing themselves with all manner of strange but always solid objects in their attempts at self-abasement and penitence. The play is set at the time of the plagues, and the Flagellants hope that their sacrifice will appease God and sort things out. But it is the troupe of unlikely clowns, led by Father Floti, who prove to be the salvation of the people, though not the cure of the plague, by bringing the hope of laughter and humour into their lives, and a reassurance of the humour of faith and the laughter and the tears of God. Holiness and humour go hand in hand, whereas holiness and humiliation that is self-inflicted and sought for seem to be self-indulgent and ultimately godless. At the end of the play, Father Floti and his troupe are conveniently dispensed with with a minimum of thanks because things have to return to normal, religion must once again be taken seriously, and the

Church must once again assume its position of power and privilege, where the first shall be first and the last last!

Yet the Church doesn't have to retreat behind the ramparts or put itself quite out of reach of the common man. The Church should be neither impregnable nor inaccessible, but rather defenceless and vulnerable. We have always wallowed in apologetics and produced tomes and tomes of arguments about the existence of God, and even more tomes in justification of all that we believe and do. We feel threatened when people on the outside of the Church find us ludicrous, our faith in God preposterous and our attempts at piety a charade. But what if instead of battening down the hatches or writing another volume or simply adopting a vastly superior and patronizing stance, we simply agreed with the assessment? What if we laid ourselves open and learned?

The Clown's Church embraces the fact that faith is absurd. It's absurd to believe that God should be born at all, never mind of a virgin in a mucky stable, and even more absurd to believe that God should die on a criminal's cross. It's absurd to believe that a man should rise from the dead, and even more absurd to believe that he is still alive and somehow living in every person in the world. It's absurd to believe that what happened two thousand years ago should have anything to do with us in today's society, and even more absurd for millions of people to base their lives on the teaching of a man of those days. The practice of our faith is equally absurd in that it might involve us helping with jumble sales and going to coffee mornings, arranging the flowers and giving out lots of service books, sitting on committees and perhaps keeping a neighbourly eye on the old lady down the road. We gather in church to sing songs and pray prayers, to wave our arms in the air and speak gibberish, fall asleep in the sermon, faint from the incense, be nice to the vicar, and promise to be there next week. It's absurd that a Church which is founded on love should be the cause of so much prejudice, violence and war, and itself be divided into countless factions and fractions. But that's where we start from and we can't start from anywhere else. If we âre laughable then let's learn to laugh at ourselves, look at ourselves anew, and then begin to laugh with joy at the wonderful absurdity of it all. The absurdity of faith isn't evidence against it, rather the contrary – the thought that only a fool would believe all that nonsense is rather encouraging! Much of what we believe is based on nonsense – it doesn't make sense in the world's terms. But we are dealing with the things of God not the ways of the world, and back we come to St Paul's realization that the foolishness of God is wiser than the wisdom of men. The leap of faith is a crazy leap into the unknown and we can either plummet or soar, but when we land, however wobbly we may feel, we find that it's a good place to be and that what had seemed absolute nonsense now makes perfect sense and is perfectly obvious!

The Clown's Church wouldn't spend its time rebuking the world or rejecting it or ignoring it. It couldn't adopt a superior stance. It would simply tease and challenge and provoke and amuse until the world changed its ways or its mind or both. It's the Church as Jester, the one who is licensed to tell the truth, to speak of the truth in outrageous ways and get away with it as nobody else could. "Look at it this way", he cries and stands on his head, turning it topsy-turvy and delighting in the new perspective while encouraging others to follow suit. Full of mischief, wit and wisdom, light on his feet and bouncy as ever, the Jester's Church would caper and point and jest, with an eye for the truth and an ear for a story that none could match. Equally at home with kings and paupers, old men and children, harlots and hierarchy, the Jester has the ability to speak to all of them in words and images that each can understand. There's something about the clown that allows him to communicate to all sorts of different people at many different levels at the same time. The Jester's Church would have that ability, that precious gift. Not everybody has the same sense of humour but the Jester's Church tries to allow everybody to get the joke so that nobody is excluded, everybody knows, and all can laugh. Suddenly the truth is accessible. Conveyed with humour, it's there on offer for all who can get the joke. However, the Jester's humour, like the truth, may be cheerful but it's never cheap.

4

Vulnerability and Playfulness

CHEAP AND CHEERFUL CLOWNING is all very well and serves its purpose, as long as you don't expect too much from it. But true clowning is costly. It is costly because it is founded upon vulnerability and playfulness, and the best clowns are those who can not only play quite openly in all their vulnerability but who can also play with their vulnerability too. It's the vulnerability of lovers who are able simply to be themselves with each other because of their love. It's the vulnerability of children in their readiness to do anything, accept anyone, and know nothing of fear. It's the vulnerability of those who have the strength to allow themselves to be weak for therein lies their fun and fulfilment. Clowning may be costly but it has its compensations!

One of the things that my clown does is to play with failure. I attempt to make a sheet of newspaper disappear by tearing it in half, and then tearing it in half again and again, completely losing track of how many pieces I'm tearing it into. But children are happy to help out an incompetent who can't add up, even if he is rather stupid. We choose magic words, blow a magic blow, and with all the confidence in the world I chuck all the pieces up in the air proclaiming that the newspaper has disappeared. Of course it hasn't and the pieces shower down upon me. The expectation has been that it will disappear because clowns can do anything, clowns can do magic, or whatever. But

69

there's a great delight in my failure because the audience can identify with someone who not only fails but fails publicly and really doesn't seem to mind. The clown reminds us that we're allowed to fail, that we can learn from failure, laugh at failure and move on. And if the clown fails at the next trick too then we move on again until in the end he succeeds and everybody cheers – and are themselves cheered in the process. In a society that is geared to success, even success at all costs, the clown is a necessary counterbalance to that mentality. Here stands a walking disaster, a happy failure, a total misfit who is yet capable of all things and seems to be in touch and tune with things that others never even dream of.

But of course it can go wrong and does go wrong if we lose that element of playfulness – the weak remain weak if they're not happy in their weakness and cannot play with it and in it. As a clown I often used to get beaten up by children, and there are often one or two children who can be quite vicious with punches and kicks. Because I wear big clown boots children love to stamp on my feet to see if they are really that size. In other words, they know that I am real if I hurt. There was a time when I allowed kids to do that to me and just suffered in silence – a misguided idealism thought it right to allow them to fulfil their needs at my expense. But nobody needs to inflict violence on somebody else, whatever their pent-up frustrations, and nobody wants or needs martyrs when martyrdom is quite uncalled for! Reducing the violence to slapstick is more what is needed. Pretending to stamp back on their feet brings play into the frame, transforms the original intent, and makes playmates of the aggressor and his intended victim. On a practical level, once play is established not just the rules but the game can easily be changed.

Children are very perceptive when it comes to pin-pointing weakness in others, whether children or adults, and are happy to go for the kill. That instinct needs no encouragement from anyone, least of all clowns. Children need to see how far they are allowed to go, and they don't necessarily want to go as far as you let them! Clowns need to nurture the child's sensitivity to weakness but try to ensure the response is one of sympathy and compassion not one-upmanship or opportunism. The clown embodies and offers a world where different rules apply, a world that has been turned upside down and inside out, a playful world where the only rules are the law of love. It's a place where everybody wins and everybody loses, all at the same time. It's the world where the first are last and the last first, so that when the first become last they become first again! But nobody's counting, because everybody counts – everyone is important and each is loved.

The clown's world is a pointer to the playfulness of the Kingdom of God. When Jesus warned the disciples that "unless you turn round and become like children, you will never enter the kingdom of heaven" (Matthew 18:3), he was talking to a group of people who were beginning to take themselves too seriously. They had been given power and authority and had taken it in their stride, but they found it difficult when things didn't quite work or when too much was expected of them. They had just found themselves unable to heal an epileptic boy and it had begged a few questions of them. Failure usually does beg a few questions. One of the questions must have been how people could take them seriously when they couldn't even heal an epileptic boy. Their authority was being called into question.

Soon after this along came the sons of Zebedee with their mother who asked the favour of her sons being granted the seats on either side of Jesus in his Kingdom. But that wasn't what it was all about. They could and would share his cup, and there was no doubt it wasn't all going to be a bed of roses, but they just had to get on with serving each other, playing as equals, answering the needs and demands of love. They didn't have to worry about the organization or the hierarchy or anything else because others would sort all that out. It was playtime and they had but to invite others out to play. There would come a time when their playleader would have to go away, and then they would have to do it for themselves. As long as they remained like children, with all their enthusiasms, their laughter and tears, their thirst for learning, and their accepting ways, all would be well.

The Kingdom was a banquet, a party where all anyone has to do is enjoy themselves and to which all are invited. Or again it was a mustard seed or buried treasure or a precious stone. The Kingdom was the stuff of stories and adventures, of feasting and fun, precious and playful. While the Pharisees and hypocrites were content to go on playing Blind Man's Bluff, the Kingdom was more like Pass the Parcel, where yet another layer has to be stripped off each time the music stops, but still the music goes on until the real prize is found right at the heart of it. The sons of Zebedee, like many before them and many more since, had been deceived by a prize in the outer wrappings and thought the game over. Judas decided he couldn't play at all. It seemed to Judas that Jesus not only wasn't taking him seriously enough, he wasn't even taking himself seriously nor even the task in hand. But in topsy-turvydom where kings ride on donkeys and clowns are always crucified, different criteria are needed. Judas decided to ruin the game by taking the ball home because it belonged to him – if they weren't going to play it his way then they weren't going to play at all. In so doing he played it God's way; but then he wasn't to know that because he thought he'd stopped the game.

Clowns haven't got time to take themselves seriously, there are too many games to play. The clown sees everything as if for the first time and responds accordingly. Blessed by that naïvety and the newness of things, he never knows what's going to happen next, but it never deters him. Unencumbered by past histories or politics, he is open to all possibilities. Present him with a simple problem and he seems to have all sorts of trouble solving it. Yet, more likely than not, for him they're not problems but opportunities, and there are all sorts of games to be played along the way. And maybe he's solved the problem anyway by transforming it from a problem into a game, and we wonder why we thought it was such a problem in the first place. The clown represents the triumph of hope over experience. It is a hope that hurts because it is grounded in the clown's vulnerability, but it is the genuine article.

Being vulnerable means taking risks, maybe with one's life or lifestyle, but certainly with oneself. We all build up patterns of behaviour and daily routines that are safe places to be because they provide the security of familiarity and home comforts. Our character has developed in fits and starts and we've ended up with what we are thanks to a mixture of self-repression and society approval, as well as genes and circumstance. To explore our vulnerability is to be very unBritish because it means getting to know our emotions again, especially the ones that we aren't too keen on, rediscovering maybe the passion and idealism of our youth as well as the playfulness of our childhood, and trying to jettison some of our security blankets as we grasp new opportunities. Part of the job of finding the clown in you is to discover whether that clown is angry or sad or happy or proud or whatever. To be a clown is not to stick on that red nose and "Smile, please", as many people presume and demand; it's to be true to your own foolish self. That might be the complete opposite of what you have become in "real life", and indeed the opposite is a good place to begin the search, but somewhere inside there's a clown waiting to come out to play. It's important to know that he does want to come out to play because otherwise it might be a bit scary and we don't want to let the cat out of the bag, never mind skeletons from the closet. Yet there's nothing to be frightened of in giving oneself away – there comes an enjoyment in the giving, and nothing is lost if we only let go. There's a clown in there, not a monster, and sometimes we can hear him coming a mile off, sometimes he's suddenly there beside us, but the clown is a vulnerable lover and he's good to be with – he's good to be!

To learn to be vulnerable might be to experiment with clothes that are different in colour and style from what you've always worn, or clothes that are wildly inappropriate or simply unfashionable – we behave differently and people respond differently to us. Clown costumes certainly fit the bill, but we can try it less obviously too! To learn to be vulnerable might be to experiment with what we could be rather than to make do with what we've become. That may mean doing those things that you've always wanted to but never dared, maybe for reasons of finance or social approval or family or business commitments or whatever the convenient excuses have always been. To learn to be vulnerable might be to express our anger or fears or grief or exhilaration or wonder or whatever it might be that somehow has always seemed a bit excessive or unnecessary or a bit too frightening to fit into cosy and mundane worlds. Having got to know those parts of us then we can play with those emotions and they lose their nightmarishness, and bring colour and spontaneity and even a bit of daring unpredictability into our lives. To learn to be vulnerable is to be prepared to be hurt, for that is the cost of loving – you can't have love without hurt. Sometimes it's only the hurt of grazed knees or dented pride, and sometimes it's the agony of a broken heart. Yet love can still kiss it better and be warm in its embrace, healing and hurting too, ever patient, giving all the time and space that's required.

On the whole I guess we would rather be vulnerable in private because that seems safer to begin with, and it's true that we need safe places to explore in. A workshop is a gathering of people who come to participate in a learning experience under the tutelage or direction of an "expert". They are thus safe places in this respect because we join with kindred spirits and there is a trust and mutual encouragement that we might not find elsewhere. It also helps to come together with strangers because it protects our anonymity and we're less burdened by our own history, we're less worried about what others might think in the future; and yet we part as friends who know far more about each other after a couple of days than people back home whom we have known for years. Those whom we spend a lot of time with sometimes know the least about us, but that may be because that's the safest way to have a relationship with someone. Workshops provide a safety net rather than a safety curtain. A safety net is a reassuring place to fall into when risks are being taken, so that they don't seem quite so life-threatening after all; a safety curtain protects us from any risks, real or imagined, and provide us with a convenient screen to shield us from ourselves and from other people.

Being vulnerable in public is the stuff of dreams and nightmares. I used to have a classic dream where I was the ballboy for the FA Cup Final at Wembley Stadium, with a crowd of a hundred thousand packed in, but somehow I didn't have any clothes on – everybody else did! There weren't any places to hide and there wasn't a fig leaf in sight! Or again, more recently, I'd climb into the pulpit to preach a sermon and find that my script had vanished and that I had absolutely nothing to say. Yet the voyage to vulnerability charts the discovery that there is far more to you than meets the eye, and far more in you than you ever thought. It's the digging up of buried treasure and talents, the revelation of untold natural resources. We can only be brave enough to live and behave as though there's nothing to hide once we are fairly confident that there's nothing much that's left hidden, and what there is is less than frightening! Only a fool attempts it, of course, but the risk is a worthwhile one – and risks must be worthwhile rather than simply gratuitous.

One of the things that I sometimes encourage people to do in church is to share the Peace. Lots of congregations do it, where people shake hands with and greet each other in appropriate ways, strictly speaking offering the Peace of the Lord to each other in the process. It varies enormously from place to place as to how much warmth and gusto it has, ranging from the very formal with minimal movement to a complete free-for-all with absolute bedlam. What I as clown suggest to the congregation is that, instead of shaking hands with people in the normal way (which nobody likes anyway because you don't know where they have been!), they have three choices: they can shake their hands above their heads, shouting "Cooeee", or they can shake their hands in front of them imitating the gestures and sound of a seal, or they can stand up (which is why they have to stand up for the Peace), bend over and waggle their hands behind them like a dog's tail, shouting "No, no, no!" Everyone must choose one of these (the first is always the most popular) and then, when given the cue, all we have to do is to find people doing it differently from us and greet as many of them as we can. It's utter stuff and nonsense, and some people love it while others can't cope with it at all. But what it does allow is for people to be playful, foolish and vulnerable in public with approval, indeed encouragement. Very often I can see people eyeing each other rather tentatively as I'm showing them what to do, just checking out how far other people might go before deciding for themselves. When it works, everybody goes for it with a certain wild abandon, before inevitably realizing where they are and reverting to type, especially when the organ starts for the beginning of the next hymn. But it changes the service: it changes the expectations of the congregation and the whole feel of the place. People have been happy to make fools of themselves in church, to play, to move, to feel and to react. We then begin to worship with more of ourselves – maybe not with all our heart, mind, soul and strength, but at least with more of ourselves than hitherto.

One of the clown's tasks is to help adults to play. It is best to have an all-age audience or congregation because the children give the adults licence to play. If the children are enjoying it, then the adults feel that they can join in too. They may excuse it on the grounds of just joining in "for the sake of the children", or they might secretly hope that nobody notices or minds them hooting and laughing and shouting at the back because they'll be drowned by the children or because the focus is on the children anyway. But that giving of permission is important. It's the same as any parent and child. A woman who at work is the most straight-laced, super-efficient, even enormously dull person in the office is reduced to a blathering idiot rolling on the floor when she gets home to her tantrummy toddler or cooing baby. A man who goes everywhere by car and hasn't taken any exercise in years is suddenly an eager footballer when occasion and child demand it. They are given the licence to play, a licence that many yearn for. Countless are the people who look forward to parenthood because that will give them the chance to do the things they haven't been allowed to do since their own childhood, and some of the things their deprived childhood didn't allow at all. They can go to the zoo and the swimming pool and the swings, buy train sets, dolls' houses and computer games, and get away with all sorts of things because "we're only playing". It is a glorious liberty. I'm sure some friends of ours only come round to play with the children's toys – they don't really want to see us at all until they have had a go with the trains and built some Lego houses! The reverse may also be true — some people do claim to hate children but there can't be any playful people who do. I wonder if the churches that don't welcome or want children in their services are simply frightened of being asked or even tempted to play . . .

If the whole congregation begins to play then worship really takes off, it lifts off and enters the world of mystery and transcendence. One of the things that grounds worship before it even starts is people taking themselves too seriously, and "religious" people are sadly rather prone to it. But if their attention can be shifted away from themselves and their concern about their own appearance and performance and their standing and status with God, then their fellow worshippers and even the Holy Spirit can begin to squeeze into the picture. You can't begin to take God seriously if you take yourself seriously, because self always gets in the way and takes priority and precedence. Prayer isn't a top-level board meeting between two frightfully important people, it is a form of play in which friendship is formed and trust is forged, and it must be entered upon playfully lest it be reduced to the muttered mumbo-jumbo that the world presumes it to be already. If prayer is embarked upon with too earnest and self-centred intent it becomes a merely human activity, an earthbound phenomenon. Pray playfully and we enter a world where different rules apply. Prayer isn't straightforward and yet it is simple. The great paradox of prayer is that we pray to a God who is already within us and who prays with us and through us; he knows exactly what we need and want even before we do, yet he still wants and needs our prayers, still wants and needs us, still wants and needs people to play with – people with whom and through whom he can make things happen. In play, as in prayer, anything can happen!

The world of prayer is the clown's realm. It is the world of miracle and truth where all that the clown touches is transfigured and transformed by the irrepressible hope of laughter and the deep compassion of his tears. The exercise of prayer is marked by its sense of expectancy but is devoid of demand – preferential treatment and preferred objectives run contrary to the rules and ethos of the game. In prayer the clown within us unites with the divine in praise and adoration, penitence and thanksgiving, laughter and tears. Prayer is to be lived and revelled in rather than said nicely. Yet maybe too often we end up saying our prayers rather than praying, clinging to the wreckage of dull custom rather than sailing off to uncharted waters. The prayer of the vulnerable lover is not a shopping list or a news bulletin or choice titbits of half-baked theology or moralistic judgements; the prayer of the vulnerable lover leaves everything in God's hands, starts from scratch, and offers "Here am I, send me!" The prayer of the vulnerable lover has no strings attached, no limits to its intention, and no advice to proffer. The prayer of the vulnerable lover derives from a willingness to play, a longing for the Kingdom, and a simple love of God. In prayer the Clown enters the imagination of men's hearts and drags them out to play. The traditional invitation to prayer is a sombre "Let us pray", with all its grave connotations and implicit instructions about posture. We all know exactly what to expect, when to join in (if at all), how long it will take, and so on. But what if the invitation were rather "Let us play!" . . .?

5

A Question of Status

ONE OF MY FAVOURITE CARTOONS, that Chic once created for me for our old parish magazine when I was a curate, was of a clown and a bishop skipping along together. The clown was in front wearing a classic conical hat with three large pom-poms down the middle of it, followed by the bishop who was wearing a mitre with three identical pom-poms. The caption was the bishop's enthusiastic admission that "Yes, they do make a difference!" The mitre is a great symbol of status in the Anglican Church at least. It seems a strange piece of headgear for a shepherd of souls and a servant of the Church. When I was on the staff of Southwark Cathedral I spent a fair amount of time in services holding bishops' mitres for them during the bits when they weren't supposed to be wearing them e.g. when they were saying prayers, although not when they were pronouncing God's blessing. It's a pretty good status symbol if it needs an extra person to hold it for you, and having that extra person simply reinforces its authority. But if we were to add three pom-poms to that mitre, we suddenly enter the dimension where the first shall be last and the last first.

The clown has no concept of status apart from recognizing it when he sees it and debunking it where necessary. The clown can play with status because it isn't important to him at all. He can sit alongside the mighty in their seats or he can bring them down if he chooses to.

He stands alongside the lowest of the low, touching the untouchables, mixing with old and young, healthy and sick. He is at home with everyone because he is Everyman and all can identify with him. There can be no status because status is a barrier, a hurdle to cross, and you have to know the rules of the game called "Decorum and Propriety". Status maintains the status quo, and that's not what the clown wants at all, because it denies opportunities and takes no risks. Give the bishop his pom-poms on his head and we begin to turn the Church on its head too. We can move away from hierarchical structures towards the people's Church, even the priesthood of all believers. If the first are last and the last first we remove all sorts of devious ambitions and intentions in one fell swoop. When the bishop admits the actress gets to heaven before he does, then we all have to start thinking again!

The bishop's other great status symbol is his chair, his "cathedra". His chair is so important that it has to have a cathedral built round it to house it. It's his throne, a wonderful symbol of kingly authority. When a bishop becomes bishop of a diocese in the Anglican Church he is enthroned. Mervyn Stockwood, who ordained me, boasted at one of his many farewells to the diocese that he was the last of the Prince Bishops, and many have been proud to be so in years past. It does seem strange that a bishop's standing is determined by his sitting, his status by his seat! But what happens when princes want to be paupers? What if every bishop at his enthronement had a clown to lead him in, a clown to hand him his symbols of status, a clown remaining by his side, reminding him and the congregation of the other half of himself, proclaiming not just that he is only human but that he is also foolish in the best as well as every sense of the word? Just as king and jester are complementary and each is incomplete without the other, so bishop and clown might equally be the same. The clown puts the bishop's status and task into perspective. He reminds him of the foolishness of what he is about to attempt as well as the absurdity of the expectations placed upon him. But he also earths him in his humanity while yet pointing him to divine dimensions. What if at the high point of the enthronement service it was the clown who took his seat on the cathedra, under the pretext of warming it up for his master, of course? What a powerful statement that might be. It might say something about his role as the messenger and mediator of and for God. It might say something about his being the licensed truth-teller, the observer of society and the Church, the vulnerable lover. It might say something about power and powerlessness. It might say all sorts of things, including "There but for the grace of God goes Everyman".

Perhaps the best bishops have been those who have been blessed with fools as chaplains . . . In the circus the clown's job is to be the glue that holds everything together. If anything goes wrong, the clown steps in to cover. If things need shifting between acts then the clown takes the focus, so that other things can get set up. He keeps reappearing, full of wit and wisdom, bouncing off the ringmaster, keeping him and everyone else in their place. We all know the clown is really in charge and it's him that we come to see. Without the clown the circus falls apart – it loses its focus, its meaning and its sense of perspective. It becomes pointless – full of stunts but empty in purpose. There's no coherence. If the bishop has a clown with whom to work in harness and tandem, then he can be the glue that holds the diocese, if not the Church, together, endowing it with sense and meaning, bringing wit and wisdom, and providing a natural focus of authority and unity. As with Lear and his fool, so the roles of the bishop and his chaplain are in a sense reversible and interchangeable, and nobody's quite sure who's in charge. One or the other can play Whiteface to the other's Auguste so they take it in turns to get the browbeats and slapsticks. They take it in turns to lead and be led, bowing to each other's inspiration and instinct. Crying with mirth, madness or misery, they are a redoubtable double act who are yet two halves of a solo performance. Ultimately it is the bishop who has the final say, the authority to cut off the chaplain's head, but woe betide the bishop who abuses that privilege!

A suffragan (assistant) bishop can't fulfil the same function because his status is too akin to that of his diocesan bishop. A contrasting status is the most effective, such as the classic master-and-servant relationship. But it depends on the see-saw relationship, where one goes down to let the other one up before being raised up himself. See-saws are boring if they stay stable in the middle, perfectly balanced. They are fun if they bounce and bump. If one person is obviously weightier than the other, his exertions and efforts at getting himself up can be hilarious, whereas to see the lightweight becalmed with no hope of self-help can be delightful. But then ways must be found to change the situation. It's a question of learning how to play with status.

We are all conscious of status most of the time. We have adopted postures and gestures and manners that pronounce our chosen status. Much of our conversations and actions revolves around establishing our status. High status people like to put other people down because it makes them feel even higher. Low status people are happy to be put down because they feel it's all they deserve. Middle status people are more difficult, but they tend to know their place, deciding who is above them and who below. Society works on that kind of status principle. But when the status player comes along, who sits lightly to status, changing his own status at whim, then everyone else has to watch out. The status player is happy to raise the status of someone else, even if he or she doesn't want it raised. So perhaps he compliments her on her work or him on his appearance, or is grateful for their advice. Alternatively he can cut a high status person dead and thus lower his status. In these situations the status player is in control because only he knows the rules of the game. The best status games are when everyone knows the rules and everyone climbs happily onto the see-saw.

We need to recognize the games we all play for real in real life first and to recognize our own preferred status. It's easier to see it in others before applying it to ourselves, so let's wheel in three bishops. The high-status bishop is our prince bishop who likes to remain on his pedestal, unapproachable, surrounded by a coterie of sycophants who continually raise his status and keep other people away. Seen only by appointment, if at all, he is the chairman of all committees that he sits on, although he makes it clear that his word is decisive and final. He may well strike terror into the hearts of many, and that suits him just fine.

The low-status bishop, on the other hand, is always apologetic about being a bishop at all, hates wearing anything that might give the game away, obviously has little control over anything that happens in the diocese, heeds the advice of anyone regardless of the wisdom or source of that advice, and is largely seen as quite ineffectual and something of a burden to the diocese. He probably thinks he is being terribly humble and virtuous and wise, which only goes to show that you can't play low status if you agree to be a bishop of the Church!

The middle-status bishop might well be a suffragan bishop, who can lord it over some people but only the ones in his own area of responsibility or those who don't know any better. Meanwhile he is still subservient to his own diocesan bishop, and probably umpteen of the committees and synods and diocesan staff that actually make the decisions in lots of places. It can be an impossibly frustrating place to be.

These are all caricatures, but caricatures are inevitable when status is clung to. Christians are caricatured as hypocrites when they take the high moral ground and cling to its status; or as woolly-minded liberals who sit firmly on the fence when they cling to the middle ground despite their own reservations and beliefs; or as terribly pious or nauseatingly goody-goody when their vain attempts at being 'umble continue to be totally unconvincing. Playing with status allows us to be true to ourselves and thus be convincing, while freeing us to be spontaneous and appropriate in status. Status only matters in the context of the game – it matters that we get it right in any given situation and every different relationship, but it's not the end of the world if we don't quite hit it off.

If we look in the New Testament, St Paul was a great status player, happy to be a Jew with Jews, a slave with slaves, a Pharisee with Pharisees, and so on. Perhaps his preferred status had always been high in the past, as a Pharisee and persecutor of Christians, but that all changed on his conversion. His letters are full of examples of him raising and lowering both his status and the status of those he is writing to. They are full of humour, abounding with rebukes and compliments, self-pity and self-abasement quickly followed by self-aggrandizement and self-justification. John the Baptist quickly recognized the see-saw principle in his determination that he must decrease so that Jesus could increase. While John could say of Jesus that he was not worthy even to lace up his shoes, Jesus could also say of John that there was no son born of a mother who was greater than John the Baptist. Jesus raises the status of people like the Samaritan woman at the well and Zacchaeus, and lowers the status of others like the rich young man and even Pontius Pilate. Poor old Peter has his status raised on being told he is the rock on which the Church will be built, only to have it lowered again as he is told he is the devil himself and a stumbling block.

A standard status game exercise in a workshop is one where people are divided into pairs and then encouraged to compliment each other in turn, thereby raising each other's status. What they soon find is that they run out of compliments, so the next stage is to demean oneself as a way of complimenting the other, and so the see-saw principle begins. This can be quite an uplifting experience in every sense, especially for those who are not accustomed to either giving or receiving compliments and who thus discover the spine-tingling possibilities of both. It has got to be played with, however, and it's no use being terribly earnest or worrying about the truthfulness of compliments.

In the same vein, the pair are then encouraged to insult

each other, not with truthful insults like "Big Ears" or "Spoilt Brat", but with impossibly rude and lewd curses which they wouldn't dream of using. When it warms up it's quite liberating! Using gibberish is another way of doing it because it's not so much the actual words that matter but the attitude and the response. The one who is insulted has to react to the insult so that there is a real interplay going on. In gibberish a good way to work it is that you repeat the last word or two words that have been thrown at you, and then offer more! Another fun way is to use ecclesiastical curses. In a show called *Picking Up the Pieces*, Darren Hoskins and I are two monks, and in one scene he bears down on me, prodding me in the chest and pushing me over, calling me "You pew, you nave, you font, you crypt, you pulpit!" Then I can take no more and I start to fight back, but enjoying the game of the insults. So I call him "You priest's girdle, you gothic clerestory, you chancel step, you rotten little lady chapel, you triple-vaulted hammer-beamed ceiling!" Then Darren can take no more and exclaims, "I've never been so buttressed in my entire life", and a slapstick fight begins. Playing with insults is fun because the words can't hurt if we're not worried about our status and don't cling to precious images of ourselves. Jesus was outrageous in his insults of the hypocrites and Pharisees, relishing each insult for all it was worth. The insults struck home because the Pharisees couldn't play the status game and therefore couldn't trade insults for fear of losing face as well as status.

A good master-servant game is to choose one of the group as the master, with total authority over everyone else, including the ultimate power of life and death. If a servant doesn't please him, for any reason at all, he is killed. The master has therefore to be quite autocratic and can be quite whimsical. The game is played with the master issuing instructions which the servant has to obey. The secret to being a servant is to be accessible and available, to grant the master the requisite amount of space, and to answer his real needs not the presumed ones. The servant soon discovers what the master likes and doesn't like and must act accordingly. The servant mustn't get in the way or detract attention or focus from the master, he mustn't challenge or deny him because the master is always right. Like every good clown he always says "Yes" and complies with instructions. It is best to give each servant three "lives". Some people adore being servants, others are quite surprised at how much they enjoy the power of being the master.

There are variations on the game. The servants become courtiers who must please the King in order to be allowed to stay in the court – this demands the courtiers offering themselves or their services rather than responding to instructions, so they do have to be aware of the wants and needs and moods of the King, and lower or raise his status accordingly. Or again, the master is a bishop and the rest are his clergy and they must please the bishop to be allowed to stay in the diocese. The trick is not to approach the "Bishop" as if he was the real one, but to play the game and know your life depends on pleasing this bishop in front of you!

A good exercise for establishing your own preferred status is to make everyone mingle in a fairly small space. The only instruction is that you have to keep moving and that you have to establish eye contact with everyone as you come across them. The high status people will try to stare the others out, the medium status will engage eyes and then decide what to do next, the low status will hardly look at all and glance away as soon as possible. There is a physical correlation too, where the low status might shuffle, fidget and be downcast, the high status will strut confidently in perfect control of their bodies, the middle status in all their up-and-downness are neither so sure nor so subservient as they seem. Having established your own, you then have to try another status, which is usually quite difficult, not least because it means breaking the habits of a lifetime. But again it can be quite a revelation. I have always slipped into low status, given a choice. My clown was a childish one who would always go pigeon-toed and tongue-tied if allowed to – the naughty schoolboy type. But that was too easy. Now I've learned how to play with the different levels and it's much more rewarding for me and for an audience. Slipping into outraged high status can get me out of, as well as into, all sorts of trouble!

Another status game is to have a line of six people in hierarchical order: bishop, archdeacon, vicar, curate, churchwarden, layperson. Each must respond appropriately to the others, but especially to those next to him or her. So when the bishop tells the archdeacon that he's lost his mitre, the archdeacon responds sympathetically to the bishop but then turns in rage to the vicar, who gets quite flustered with the archdeacon but is quite calm with the curate, who panics about the bishop and pleads with the churchwarden, who takes it out on the layperson whose fault of course it wasn't! Messages can be sent in either direction and problems arise from any quarter. Add a child or a local tramp or a non-churchgoer on to the end and the dynamic changes. If the Tramp asks what a mitre is and at once begs for a change of clothes and a pair of shoes, he immediately raises his own status and lowers the status of all that has gone before by putting it into perspective and himself into focus. Somewhere along the line the problem has to be dealt with, but the news will still reach the other end, especially if no one has yet found the mitre. As soon as it comes to an impasse or solution another problem arises or a new instruction is sent. There are times when the layperson on the end never gets a look in and the bishop never ever hears the whole truth, but what's new!

What people need to learn is to be equally adept in each of the positions. While a person might like being bishop best of all, he's got to be able to be the layperson and the vicar too, to know what it's like to be in their shoes and to play with their status. When the bishop suddenly misses out all the middlemen and talks directly to the layperson or the Tramp, there is a maximum status gap which the two of them need to close sufficiently to be able to communicate. Standing on dignity is hopeless – sometimes it needs to be stamped on very firmly indeed!

It seems to me that it would be a good idea to resurrect the tradition of the Feast of Fools in our churches and allow its anarchy to purge us of our pretensions. What if a girl was made bishop for the day and a Sunday School took over the diocesan office? There could be a service with milk chocolate buttons instead of wafers, and solemn readings of Enid Blyton (Old Testament), *Thomas the Tank Engine* (Epistle) and Roald Dahl (Gospel). Custard pies could be exchanged at the Sharing of the Peace. The altar could be used for selling jumble, and crockery and kitchen utensils be tastefully arranged in vases. The clergy would have to be patronized in the vestry till the service was over, but they could be allowed in afterwards as long as they kept quiet. There would be songs that everyone knew and enjoyed. The choir would have to stand on their heads and hum, ignoring the fact that their robes hid their faces but not much else besides! There would be fireworks from every church tower, graveyards and gravestones would be decorated and dressed, and a bonfire be made of church hats. The elderly would be honoured and children listened to. There would be puppets in the pulpit, punch in the font, and balloons and party games for all ages. It could all take place on April Fool's Day, or All Fools' Day, and everyone could be reassured that it was all a practical joke and that normal service would be resumed as soon as possible.

But that whole inversion of status might provide us with a Church that allowed the first to be last and the last first, that didn't take itself so seriously that God never got in on the status line, and which recognized the foolishness of God to be wiser than human wisdom, even if it meant confirming that the Kingdom of God belongs to children and those who are childlike. It would only work if that which we lampoon we really hold dear, and those who cherish our churches from afar might just be offended, but it would be worth it. If bishops could be clowns and clowns bishops, then anything could happen.

6

Clown Character References

PART OF THE DISCOVERY OF your own clown within you is the freedom it gives you to express the level of status that you have always secretly desired or that you simply enjoy and haven't had the opportunity to use. While you might be quite low status in your real life, your clown might be impossibly high status and you can revel in it! Just as some actors will say that the clue to a character lies in the way he walks, so the clue to your clown lies in the way that your clown moves.

Let's take ourselves into a workshop situation – a safe and creative place to try and discover that clown in you. After a few games and warm-up exercises I encourage people to walk around the room "normally", to relax and ignore the fact henceforth that this is an artificial situation. Then we change the pace and motive and style. So they move as if they're late, then late but trying not to let anyone notice they're hurrying, then dawdling or daydreaming. Suddenly we're on a beach with sand in our toes, or scurrying over hot pebbles, or wading in the sea, or tramping through long grass. We're creeping into the house late at night, taking somebody by surprise, or we're a slow-motion action replay of a goal at football. We're pigeon-toed, or we've got splayed feet or flat feet. We walk on heels, goose step, or high kick. There is, of course, a whole range of possibilities, but the art is to believe that you are in the situation offered or to become a character that walks in a certain way because then it takes on a life and reality of its own and becomes convincing. It also breaks our own habits, albeit briefly, and allows us to experiment with these other ways.

Attacking it from another angle, there are physical ways of moving that signal the character of the person and his predominant emotions. If I move as if there was a piece of string pulling me along by my forehead, so that my forehead is leading me on, I am likely either to move slowly and rather slow-wittedly, or to stomp forwards aggressively. If I'm led by my eyes there is either an eagerness to rush forwards and discover something, or a wide-eyed fear that resists and wants to move me backwards and away. Led by the nose I become inquisitive and jerky in movement. Led by the chin I become snooty and arrogant, or simply a daydreamer with my head in the clouds. Puffing out my chest I become quite military and stride with confidence, while a woman is not ashamed to carry all before her. Led by the stomach I am obese and disgusting, or heavy and pregnant, or grossly content if heavy-footed. Led by the pelvis I can be quite sluttish or cocky or sensuous – there is great power in the pelvis but most of us are too embarrassed to use it! Led by the knees I become frail and vulnerable, a toddler or an old lady, easily unbalanced.

This is a difficult exercise because the difference in nuance and posture is sometimes slight, and it does nothing for some people. It needs space and time. It is best to try different speeds to see which feels right and then allow yourself to see what it feels like to walk in that particular way. Sometimes it helps to greet other people in order to see how this type of character interacts. But you need to turn and mix and mingle rather than all go round in the same circle at the same speed. What people find is that some of those gaits are extremely difficult or alien to them, while there are others that they can slip into quite naturally and easily, and it's the latter that we need to hold on to − those are the ones the clown can use.

One exercise I often use is to have a sort of "Miss World" competition where the group are both the audience and the contestants. In turn each one has to parade along the catwalk, stop in the middle, look at the audience, convince them that he or she is the sexiest thing in the world on two legs, and then move on. To begin with the whole idea is horribly embarrassing because it inevitably means the pelvic walk and a confident swagger. Those who can't cope with it provide cameos and stylized caricatures, and that adds to the fun. Those who are prepared to go for it find it unnerving but exhilarating, because if it is done with conviction so that the "contestant" actually believes he or she is the sexiest person in the world, it works − and the applause as well as the intake of breath is thunderous! It doesn't work if it is hammed, but it also fails if the posture and gait are wrong. You aren't sexy if you walk with pigeon-toed embarrassment or with your chin in the air. And even if you get the gait and feel right, you then have to communicate what you feel with your eyes and be eye-catching. That's another dangerous game because we assume people can see right through us, through the windows of our soul, and we'd rather close the curtains. But we need that contact to convince, and we need it in order to feed off other people, to react and respond accordingly. It's a vulnerable place to be. In every way it is an exercise in "going for it", and if you pull out of it it isn't going to do anything for anyone. A variation on this exercise is that each person rushes on, stops, and announces, "Hey everyone, I've got some wonderful news", before charging off again. The way some people do it is quite implausible and we couldn't care what the news is, but others arrest our attention and whet our appetite and imagination, and we want to hear what they have to say. For Christians who wish to proclaim the Good News it's an illuminating exercise.

Communication of conviction is important but so is the communication of our emotions, of how we feel and who we are. A message is hollow and empty if it carries with it no feeling nor any clue as to who the sender is and what his sentiments and intentions might be. It is therefore crucial to be in touch with our emotions, to have access to them and be prepared to show and share them playfully. So I ask the group to spread out and give themselves a bit of space each, and then warn them that we're going to try to explore and express some emotions.

I ask them to be happy – not just to look happy but to actually try and feel happy because that's the only way that it will communicate. To put on a plastic grin or adopt a pose that might look happy does not convince. And, as before, it has to be communicated with the eyes, so they have to look at me and communicate it. Blank eyes betray lack of feeling. Maybe the next emotion is sadness, and everybody slumps, expressing it physically as well as internally. But they have still to raise their eyes to communicate what they feel. With anger, they stiffen and stare. With fear, eyes either narrow or widen and the body goes in retreat. In loneliness, bodies curl and eyes beseech or hide. In pride, they look down their noses and feel in control. The hardest of all is love — we're not quite sure what to do and it feels hard to "fake it". Yet back we come to the Gospel we preach and the love we must show to all people. If that message is to have any reality, then we must be able to feel it and express it. Having travelled through those emotions fairly gently, we then take them more quickly but still try and feel them rather than adopt remembered poses. It can be quite exhausting especially if we're more used to suppressing rather than expressing our emotions but taking them at speed allows the element of playfulness as well as the notion of having access to them. The hope is that we find that they aren't as frightening as we feared.

What the emotions also introduce us to is the different clown characters. In happiness we find Auguste and maybe Jester, in sadness and loneliness Tramp, in anger and pride Whiteface, and in love we should find all of them. Fear can be found in all of them but it's never an overriding factor. Again we feel more comfortable with some of those emotions than others, and that again gives us the clue to what type of clown we might be. That is not to say that we are tied to the make-up and costume of those clowns, nor that you can't have an angry Auguste or a happy Tramp. It does suggest that clowns identify with our basic needs and emotions, and that those needs and emotions are found in clowns. We come back to the realization that clowns are not superficial characters but creatures of great depth and vulnerability.

Now that we have some ideas as to the status of our clown, the ways he might walk and move, and his predominant emotions, it's time to put a few pieces of the jigsaw together with the help of an important piece of costume, known in the trade as a hat. I have a large collection of hats of all sorts, e.g. sailor's hat, bowler hat, cloth caps, sombrero, berets, trilby, wedding hats, beany hats, clown wigs, awfully unfashionable hats, cub cap, etc. Some have particular connotations but others are what you make them. The good thing about a hat is that it grants character as soon as you put it on – it allows you to become someone else. Group members are encouraged to wear a hat that takes their fancy, and then to walk around the room, seeing how the hat makes them walk. As they try to establish a walk I encourage them to think what sort of person they are, how they spend their time, what job if any they've got. Then to think of a name of that character and what story he or she might have to tell, and to see how they feel.

When they are ready they come back to be an audience again, and each in turn uses their walk to get to the middle of the "catwalk", stops, introduces themself, tells us their occupation and how they feel, and then moves on. It's a simple and effective way of testing out in public what we've been brewing in private. There isn't a wrong or right about it, though it acts as a kind of quality control. Some people find it doesn't work at all, and that may be because the hat is inappropriate. It may also be that it is very difficult to create a character that quickly. The only way that we are going to get near it is by using ourselves as the resources for that character, for we have all the elements of our clown inside us. Those elements don't have to be plucked out of thin air. We don't have to try and be terribly clever. It's a matter of feeling our way towards our clown, of following instincts rather than creating images. We normally repeat the exercise, and usually people get braver and sillier about their choice of hats, and when it comes to the introductions we find people experimenting with voices too. And if they are prepared to hold us with their eyes they know for sure how they feel and can tell us accordingly, and they may discover much more about themselves too.

I rarely use greasepaint in workshops, except with children, unless we've got lots of time and it's specifically what the group want. The important thing about grease-paint is not to use too much, not to be over-elaborate, and to find the "design" that suits your face. Every face is unique, and, strictly speaking, so is every clown face. A good way to begin is to look at yourself in a mirror and make lots of faces in order to see what your face does, where the wrinkles and creases and dimples are. If you've got a big nose you need to decide whether to make it bigger or smaller, but it's a basic principle that you should use the features that you have been blessed with. Once you've done that you can start to experiment a bit, either applying greasepaint yourself or letting someone else do it for you, either by instruction or by their own impressions. The traditional colours are red, white and black, but blues and greens and other colours can be used too. It really depends on what sort of clown you've decided to be. It's no good painting a huge smiling mouth if you've discovered you're really rather a sad clown!

Without going into the finer details, there are some basic tips. If you're going to be an Auguste, you are likely to want fairly large designs on your face and it is worth drawing them in outline with an eyeliner first, rather than going straight in with a stick of greasepaint. It is then easier to decide whether the shape works or not. It is worth being symmetrical too, so that each side of the face reflects the other, so having the outline allows you to be fairly accurate and you can then fill in with your colour afterwards. It is best to start with the lightest colours first, so apply white, then red, then black. It is also worth thickening that original outline in black when you've finished so that there is clear shape and definition. Don't worry if the lines are all a bit shaky, they are bound to be. You are also unlikely to end up with the face that you had created in your imagination before you started. It takes practice to get it smart and time to get it right! Some people use a base to cover the parts of the face that haven't got greasepaint on, although I never did. It depends partly on your own complexion. As specifically Christian clowns you might want to use Christian symbols on your face. I have a cross on each cheek, but you can use fish shapes around the eyes, or an Alpha and Omega on the cheeks or whatever. But it needs repeating that it still must suit your face and make-up or it won't be effective and it therefore won't communicate.

If you're going to be a Tramp, then you need a basic stubbled beard effect which is simply achieved by rubbing in black. Some Tramps have clearly defined edges and a solid black, but I prefer the fainter effect with edges that blend into the face – it looks scruffier! I've seen female clowns with this same bearded look, which may sound bizarre but testifies to the tradition that clowns are neither male nor female, just clowns. If women don't want beards then they have to find a scruffy alternative. Quite a lot of Tramps use white rather than red for their mouths, and red or rouge should be rubbed into the cheeks to try and get the bucolic effect if you want to be a wino. Adding a bulbous nose might be effective. Depending on whether you're sad or angry or both, you will probably have to add lines to bring your eyes down. If you want to be more a gentleman of the road in all your tattered dignity, then you need to be more subtle in the make-up!

If you want to be a Whiteface, there are round tins of white that you can use, and you can then apply it with your fingers. There seem to be various schools of thought as to how much of your face, neck and head you should cover. You can just cover the "front" of your face, perhaps using a thin line around the outside to define its surround, and this might be a mime's face. You can cover the whole face and ears and neck, which seems logical because then no flesh can be seen, but some leave the neck. There is also the tradition that you don't touch the ears except for a splash of red, but that you do everything else – that's the traditional English Whiteface. Whichever way you choose, you need to rub it in and try to get it even – don't use too much and cake it on. Once you've done that it's worth patting all over it with the ends of your fingers. You then need to add a few elegant touches, perhaps a snazzy eyebrow or something on one cheek, perhaps some colour under the nose and on the lips, and it's done. This process can be helped by using a cottonbud to create the shape that you want first and then add your colour – it saves blurring. The alternative is to powder the white first and then add colours – using a small artist's brush is very effective.

Once you've applied all the greasepaint and are as happy as can be it's worth powdering your face. Use ordinary talcum powder and a powder puff or just a piece of cotton wool or even a sockful. Brush off the excess and then either dab with water or use a spray.

Those are the three traditional types but there are growing trends to combine them. So the American

Whiteface is really an Auguste with a Whiteface base, and there are increasing numbers of Tramps with half-Auguste faces. That is inevitable really when there are so many clowns around and very few working in traditional circuses! There are also lots of character clowns, who might be based on traditional clowns, but are obviously firemen or policemen or, in my case, vicars. Whereas performing clowns have always been able to change in and out of costumes to suit the particular entree or routine that they're doing, there have always been these character clowns who keep to their peculiar character and costume.

Be that as it may, if we're not using greasepaint then I produce a box of noses. These are a mixture of silly plastic noses of all lengths and shapes, together with lots of clown red noses. A nose is the simplest form of mask, it changes the face completely, and it somehow enables us to dive into foolishness rather than just dip our toe into the water. The nose, like the greasepaint, is a mask, but it is a liberating device that releases our foolishness rather than a screen which we can hide behind. Once we find the right mask or greasepaint then we find it has a life of its own as soon as we put it on because we inhabit it and allow it to live. That's one of the reasons why lots of the great clowns talk about their clown character as someone who is entirely separate from them until they put on the costume and the face. Our pursuit is to find that clown and let him loose.

Once the noses are on, we all take an amazed look at each other and realize how different we suddenly seem. Sometimes it is difficult to remember what a person really looks like now that she's wearing a huge hooked nose! One exercise that is fun is all to do with sound effects. It's quite important to get people to talk and make noises once they are in any sort of costume or mask, because if they remain silent for any length of time it is hard to break that silence. When I started clowning I found it very hard to speak. I don't think it was because I hadn't found a 'funny voice' or anything like that, it was simply that I couldn't speak. After a while I started to develop a rather manic and fairly high-pitched voice, but it wasn't always consistent! It's also something of a revelation that you don't have to use words to communicate when noises will do, and that sound effects are not as difficult as we'd always imagined.

So, I get people into a circle and thank them most sincerely for coming to the audition. While acknowledging that they are all experts in their chosen field, I have to break the news that we only need one Old Gloucester Sow for this particular production. Reassuring them that it is radio not television, each in turn gives a rendering of an Old Gloucester Sow. The round completed, we might try an audition for Grand Opera, where each has to offer a snatch of either real or imitation opera – ''Just one Cornetto'' is a favourite! This is a good one to try because so many people are embarrassed about their singing voices when they have no need to be. A number of people have been surprised by what they have been abe to produce. Another variation is to produce the sounds of a tropical rainforest. Both the opera and the rainforest can be done as communal pieces, as long as they have been tried individually first. With the opera you simply improvise. Either I or one of the group, as conductor, point to different people in turn who have to continue where the last person left off. It is best to start with a couple of the better singers! With the rainforest you can get people to close their eyes and encourage them to start quietly, and then, in tune with and conscious of the contributions of others, build up to a crescendo before quietening down again. This can be particularly evocative and moving.

Another exercise that might follow this is to build a machine together. Without noises to begin with, one person steps into the middle and becomes a working part of a machine. So he or she establishes a rhythmical movement of an arm or a leg, say. Then everyone else begins to join in, finding movements that complement what is already going on, until at last there's a big machine up and running. Once everyone is part of it then they can each try and produce a suitable sound effect to accompany their own part of the machine – it's easier to experiment with that sound effect under cover of everyone else's noise. Once that is established they can try and speed up or slow down the machine, first under direction but then trying to do it by sensing what's happening and what the whole group want. Once the machine has stopped you can start all over again, but this time you have a sound effect as soon as you start your movement. On the second machine I often find that people are more daring and that more now work together physically rather than at a safe distance from each other. The machine as well as the group is all the better for it! It is a good exercise for experiencing St Paul's concept of the body with all its constituent parts working together, each dependent on the other.

There are a couple of fun exercises that carry on that theme. The first is to try a communal juggle. Everyone has one beanbag each and at a given signal they have to lob their beanbag to the person on their left and catch the one that's coming to them. It will only work if it's done simultaneously and if everyone lobs their beanbag to the same height. If it is achieved, and that is a pretty big 'if', you try to do it twice and then three times. Then, still clutching their beanbags, everybody gets in a straight line tucked right up behind each other, with a chair behind the person at the rear. Then everybody has to sit down on the knee of the person behind them. Once they are sitting, they put their beanbag in their right hand, and at a given signal throw the beanbag from their right to their left hand and back again. It looks a bit like synchronized swimming! If they can manage that, then they try sitting in a circle, so that they don't need the chair, and they throw the beanbag to the person immediately behind. All fall down!

Once the hysteria has died down (not that these exercises need follow each other), try going back into pairs and keep both nose and hat on. The first exercise is mirroring, where one acts as a full-length mirror to the other. The idea is to reflect the other person exactly but, as in other exercises, it is the quality and the feel of the movement that is important rather than the minutest detail. So it is vital to maintain eye contact with each other, so that you know exactly what's happening. There is no point in the person looking in the "mirror" trying to catch the mirror out by sudden or bizarre movements. It is much better to use slow and more graceful movements, and perhaps movements that have a logic to them. You might decide you're in the bathroom in the morning, or doing exercises in the mirror. Lots of movements follow naturally from each other if we allow our bodies to flow. Just as the person looking in the mirror shouldn't try to catch the mirror out, so the mirror mustn't presume what's coming next. The mirror should also reflect the emotions that are going on – motion and emotion always go together. The ideal is that the two should be moving entirely in tandem and that an onlooker wouldn't know who was leading who. Nevertheless, each person should have a go at being the mirror. Some people will enjoy being the mirror more because they prefer being led, while others prefer being the person because they prefer leading. It needs taking on board and it helps us discern our status.

After the mirror exercise those who have just been mirrors all move to the side of the room while their partners walk around "normally" – as normally as they can, given that they're being watched. Each looks to see how their partner walks, noting the detail of how they hold themselves as well as the feel of it, whether it seems proud or lazy or relaxed or hurried or whatever. Then they slot in behind their partner and try to reproduce it exactly. The person might have one hand clenched and the other open, or his head wobbles, or he lists to one side, or he leans forward. Once everyone has got it, the person in front can then step out and see what his own walk looks like, before returning to the fray once more. Once the pair has been re-established, the person behind has to choose one element of his partner's walk and exaggerate it. Having done that, they can either add another exaggerated element of their partner's walk or add something of their own that complements it. Finally the people in front are allowed to step out and see what has happened to their walk. What their partners have done for them is to find a silly walk that is based on their own, and it is offered as a way for their clown to move. It may not be the way that the clown will always move, but there are times when an exaggerated walk is called for and this is another resource. The pair then swap round and start all over again.

One final exercise to round off the chapter if not this imaginary workshop is to get everyone to find a silly walk, using what they have learned about their status, emotions and character, the ways they have enjoyed moving and so on. It can be quite different from the one in the previous exercise, because nothing is sacred and carved in stone – there's much more exploring to be done yet. Once they've established a walk – like any gait, it must have a rhythm so that it's repeatable – the group is split in two at either end of the room or hall. They then use their silly walks to cross over to the other side of the hall. They're now going to work in pairs with the person who happens to be opposite them, one pair after the other. The idea is that they again cross over once, establishing their own walk but also observing their partner's walk. Then on the return journey the task is, on the moment they pass each other, to adopt their partner's walk. Once again it is the quality of the walk that's important. The more different the two walks are, the more pronounced is the change, and the more character there is in a walk, the easier it is for your partner to capture. We can learn from seeing all the other walks what works in movement, but it also teaches us how to become someone else in an instant, and that's a great gift.

These are all basic reference points for clown character that I have found useful for myself and which I have used and others have then found useful. But they are only basic starters. No one can have a magic wand, stick a red nose on you and send you off over the horizon as a perfect clown after one afternoon's work! Ultimately it's a long process that never ends because our clown grows old and matures along with us. You can only test how you're doing by going out and clowning in public, learning from your mistakes, continuing to dare to be vulnerable, and trying to respond appropriately to every individual. Some of the best clowning is purely spontaneous response to situations and people. As long as you allow people space and don't intrude on that space unless invited, you're in with a chance. You soon get to recognize who wants to play and who doesn't, and who might with a little bit of encouragement. As long as you enjoy it, they will. If you're frightened, they will be. Raise a smile, a laugh or even a tear, and it's worth all the effort.

And if you see God in their faces and hear the Holy Spirit in their laughter, then anything could happen, one day. Clowns sometimes sow seeds, sometimes they are catalysts, sometimes they're the last straw that breaks the camel's back or the last piece in the jigsaw. There's something about the clown that offers a glimpse of divine possibilities even if we aren't explicit about it. So it's important that we find the real clown in us so that others may discern it too and through that discernment glimpse those greater horizons. That's quite a responsibility and privilege.

7

Skills and Techniques

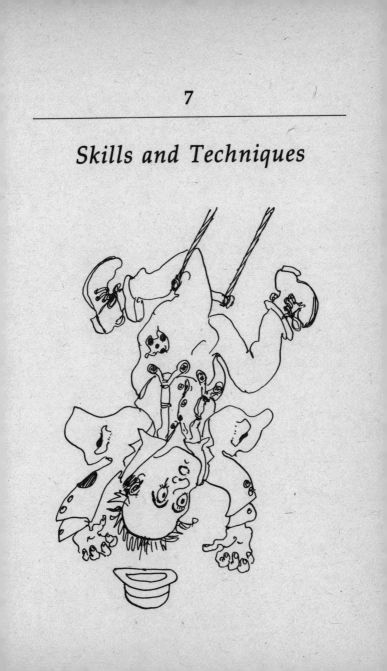

IF IT IS IMPORTANT TO FIND the real clown in you, it is equally important to be a real clown and be able to fulfil the expectations that others have of clowns. That doesn't mean that you have suddenly to be able to be the best joke-teller in the world, because that may have nothing to do with your clown and may be beyond you anyway. What you will find, however, is that people have expectations about skills and tricks and bits of stuff and nonsense, and if you can't "do something" you lose credibility.

Years ago when I had only just started clowning, a group of us went on the Easter Parade in Battersea Park, London. As it ground to yet another weary halt, we were left right underneath a man with a microphone doing a sort of commentary and jollying everyone along. Of course when he saw us, he told everybody, and then told us all to "do something". We felt a bit stymied. Having been quite happy waving and shaking hands with people and handing out balloons to the children, we were suddenly being asked to perform. One of our number attempted a rather feeble juggle, the commentator was less than impressed, and mercifully the parade moved on. It taught me an early lesson that it's no good looking good if you can't do anything good. There was no scope for me to explain carefully all about being a holy fool, and that actually I was quite funny in sketches in church, and so on! I needed to be able to show my credentials first and talk afterwards.

115

I'm neither a magician nor a balloon-modeller so I can't say anything about either skill. I have nothing against either, as long as it really is a clown doing it rather than a magician dressed as a clown, if you see what I mean. If a balloon-modeller could be wearing any costume and it wouldn't make any difference to what he did and the way he did it, then he's not being a real clown in my terms. I'd rather clowns tried a bit of balloon-modelling than balloon-modellers tried a bit of clowning. Nevertheless, doing a magic trick or making a balloon giraffe or whatever does serve its purpose, as long as we remember it's the way that it's done that's important. The beauty of clowns doing it is that it doesn't matter if it fails miserably as long as we turn it to advantage, play with the failure and carry on. Ideally the denouement should be a successful attempt or a success at a different trick or balloon model, but that isn't always possible!

What I do feel strongly about, and it was one of my main reasons for going to circus school, is that clowns should be able to master some circus skills, even if it's only three-ball juggling. In people's minds clowns are inextricably linked to the circus and there's no avoiding that. If we are seen to be skilful and therefore, however subconsciously, deriving from the magical mystical world that is the circus Big Top, then we're in business. The alternative is to be written off as "only dressed up with face paints on". Most circus skills are very simple in technique but just need a lot of practice to get them right and looking good. Whereas to find our clown is best done in community, in a group, to learn skills just needs some hard graft, working on your own most of the time. It's a bit like prayer – to begin with it seems easy and so obvious but then it needs constant discipline and practice. The other thing to remember is that you have to be able to do something well before you can do it badly or be convincing in making it look impossibly difficult. I'm not a great expert at any of them, but there are basic tips and principles. If you want to pursue any of them in greater depth you'll have to chase up other books or, better still, go and learn at skills workshops. Being shown is much better than reading and trying to work it out for yourself. It is always best to learn the right way rather than learn self-taught bad habits which have to be unlearned if progress is to be made.

The classic example of this is juggling. Lots of children learn to juggle with two balls by passing a ball from one hand to the other and then throwing. The balls thus move in a clockwise or anti-clockwise circle, and it is always the same hand that is throwing while the other hand always catches and then passes. That's absolutely hopeless if you want to juggle three balls, so you have to break the habit.

Start with one ball or, better still, a beanbag which won't bounce or roll away. Try to relax, with your feet apart and with some give in your knees, so that you can always move one way or another without difficulty. If you're stiff as a board you'll never do it! Throw the beanbag from hand to hand, but try to keep your hands just above waist level and pointing outwards about forty-five degrees. What you want to try to achieve is for the beanbag to travel in an arc or rainbow with the minimum movement of your hands. The throw is in the wrist, and the beanbag needs to be lobbed up so that it passes just above your head and lands in the other hand without that hand having to move. You mustn't try to snatch it in mid-air or grab it like a slip fielder in cricket. Just let it land in the middle of your flat hand so that it is ready to be thrown again without adjustment. You should focus on the point at the top of the arc, so that all you ever really see is the beanbag at the peak of its flight. Don't follow the flight of the beanbag from hand to hand, because when you've got more beanbags going you won't know where to look! You have to trust yourself and your body to look after the catching. Juggling is all about throwing, not about catching, so it is important throughout to get the throw right. You're bound to drop the beanbag lots of times, but that doesn't matter. If your throw is so accurate that the beanbag always lands in the flat of the other hand, you don't have to be a good catcher! I'm told that if you wanted to learn juggling in a Russian circus school you would spend three years, six hours a day, just with the one ball. That's how important the throw is!

Once you are happy with one beanbag, take a second one. All you have to do is exactly the same throw with both hands, one after the other − don't throw them at the same time. Throw the first one, and as it reaches the peak of its arc throw the second one. Both are in the air at the same time, briefly. It is important to establish a rhythm, so count it. It's worth saying out loud, "one, two", as you throw each one, or "throw, throw, catch, catch". If you persist in passing the beanbags rather than throwing them, try saying "left, right", telling your hands to throw. Hands are quite obedient really once the brain can get the message through! One thing to realize is that you have much more time than you think, so don't panic with the second one and throw it too quickly or throw it away from you. Just relax and concentrate on two good throws.

Once you've mastered two, try the third. Check which hand you normally throw first with, and put two beanbags in that hand, one in front of the other – the one in front, held by the fingers, will be the one to throw first. Once again, concentrate on the throwing not the catching, and try to establish the rhythm. To begin with, you want to try and throw each beanbag just once. If you're going to count it, try "left, right, left", telling your hands to throw. The psychological block will be to let go of the last one because you will be desperate to catch the second beanbag first. Don't! With three beanbags there is always one in the air and all you have to do is to clear the hand to which that beanbag is travelling by throwing the beanbag already in that hand to the other hand – most of the time you are actually holding two beanbags with one in each hand. If you find that you're throwing one forward it is probably out of panic, and if you can't cure it by relaxing, just juggle face in front of a wall. As the beanbag continues to hit the wall, the brain will suddenly realize how stupid this is and correct it! If you're getting backache from continually picking up the beanbags you've dropped, practise over a bed or sofa so that you haven't got so far to bend down. There is a great sense of achievement when you manage three for the first time. The next step is to try to keep going, counting the rhythm, "one, two, one, two", and continually clearing the hand to which the beanbag is travelling.

Juggling is quite obsessive because of the counting factor – you move from being able to do four throws to six to ten to twenty-seven or whatever. We are able to record our progress and achievement. Once you can do it easily there are all sorts of tricks and different ways of throwing, but you can try other books for that! More and more firms are getting their staff to learn juggling, and it's quite a craze in many places, because of its value in relaxation. It may not seem very relaxing while you're learning, but once you've got that easy rhythm going it's quite meditational. You can use it as a prayer, with a mantra. "God the Father, God the Son, and God the Holy Spirit", works to the rhythm, throwing on "God, Fa, God, Son, God, Ho, Spi". "God is Love" or "Lord, have mercy" can be used. Anything that scans, bears repetition, and is helpful as a prayer will serve the purpose. But the real bonus of juggling three beanbags is that it provides an easy illustration of the workings and understanding of the Holy Trinity!

Once you've mastered a skill you need to find ways of using it to illustrate the Gospel message. I juggle rings that double as haloes, and one of my favourite pieces is the Christmas story where the clown witnesses the birth of Jesus. He wants to offer him a gift but has nothing to offer, so in a mad moment he grabs the haloes above the heads of Mary, Joseph and the baby and starts to juggle them. When he realizes what he's done he tries to give them back, but is told to keep them. "You keep them, good clown," says Mary, "we have no need of them. People will always want us to have them but we are just ordinary people like you. You keep them, and every time you juggle them let them sing the Song of the Angels. Let people know that Jesus is born in Bethlehem of Judea, the Saviour of the World is come" . . . Juggling might also be a way of illustrating "the first shall be last, and the last first"! I'm trying to find the time to master four rings/haloes to use as a way of teaching about the four gospels. I would like to be able to pick up any objects and juggle them, because that offers more options. Once you can do tricks you could do a whole routine based on the right hand not knowing what the left is doing. There are all sorts of possibilities once you get going.

One skill that looks terribly difficult but is remarkably easy is balancing a tray of drinks, or indeed any object, on a stick. Start with a broomstick, placing the rounded end on the palm of your hand or the end of your finger, and make sure it's vertical. As long as you focus on the top of that stick you will be able to balance it because your brain gets your balancing hand to move exactly where it needs to, without you having to worry. Once you can do that, you just take a tray, find its middle as you balance it on the flat end of the broomstick, and, keeping your focus on the top of the stick, just raise it up. Add drinks and extras as you get more confident! Once you can do it on your finger, try balancing it on your chin, nose, forehead or foot. As long as you focus on the top, it will stay there. If you're trying it on your chin or nose, put your head right back. You will need to push the stick further back than you think – it may seem vertical from where you are, but it won't be! One thing to be wary of is having a tray that is either too slippery on top for the glasses or too slippery underneath for the stick. Churchwardens' staves are good for balancing, and it's alarming for the church's best offertory plate to be raised up but it is a good way of offering up our gifts!

Another piece that I've done is all about bread and wine. The invitation is to eat, drink and be merry. I start by balancing the stick, then a mug on the stick, and then some water or wine in it, and eventually let it drop so that it spills everywhere. I take a bread roll from my pocket which I tear into pieces, like the newspaper gag cited earlier – I will have done that earlier too, because that sets this up.

Of course it will not disappear, "for however much my body is broken, it is broken for you". I pick up the mug "However much my blood is spilt, it is spilt for you." The stick suddenly becomes the crosspiece of the cross before I climb into a large bag or hide somewhere, quoting "a little while and you will see me, a little while and you will not see me." After a pause I reappear juggling three bread rolls, quoting "I am the Bread of Life . . .", and I exit balancing one of those rolls on the stick, singing "I will raise him up on the last day". It's a simple but powerful way of expressing Gospel truth with skills and images, and it imbues sometimes tired words with new life and meaning.

Riding a unicycle always impresses people but it's rather a painful learning process! I'm afraid you just have to keep falling off. You need to ensure that the seat is the right height before you start. When you're sitting on the saddle, your leg should be slightly crooked when your foot is on the pedal at its lowest. Either holding on to a wall or a rail or someone, just get the feel of the unicycle by rocking gently forwards and backwards with the pedals, so that you get a sensation of the balance required. Make sure that you sit quite upright and imagine that the unicycle is part of you – you go wherever it goes and it goes wherever you go! Keep your focus up and forwards, perhaps to the target you're aiming for. There is a basic principle in all balancing that if you look down, you'll fall down. If you've got someone to lean on, let him take you for a walk, but try to rest a hand on his shoulder rather than hang on to him for dear life! In the end you just have to let go and go for it, and keep climbing back on. When you feel yourself falling, try to grab the seat as you go. This saves the unicycle being damaged too much but it also teaches you control of it, helps you learn to stay on it, and saves it careering into other people. You'll find that if you lean forwards it will travel faster, and if you take your weight back a bit it will travel slower. When you find that you have to turn corners it is achieved by a slight swivel of the hips and a lean so that your weight takes the bike round.

I've only ever used it for entrances and exits because I still can't unicycle on the spot. This involves rocking it forwards and backwards, for you can't actually keep it stationary. My favourite entrance was careering down the aisle at Bristol Cathedral with a star suspended above my crash helmet, with me desperately looking for the star – ''It's up there, it's behind you, etc.''! I'd love to see Adam and Eve on unicycles, juggling apples before the Fall. You could use a unicycle and a tricycle to tell the story of the house built on sand and the house built on rock. If you get really good and can unicycle on miniature ones and giraffes (the very tall unicycles) you could tell the story of the Tower of Babel, or do a lovely David and Goliath, or even Zacchaeus climbing higher and higher to see Jesus. More generally, perhaps the Prodigal Son having a whale of a time could see him juggling and unicycling in sparkling costume while the elder son slaves away darkly in the corner.

Moving on from the pain and perils of unicycling, a rola bola is quite impressive too. This involves you standing on a board that is balanced on a cylinder or roller, and it's quite likely to bowl you over, hence its name – roller bowler, I suppose! I use a piece of six-inch British Gas pipe (with permission!) and a three foot plank of five-ply wood with two batons screwed underneath, about two inches from each end. Again it is helpful to have somebody's shoulder to rest on, but you can use a rail or wall or the back of a sofa. It's beneficial to practise on carpet because the roller will move more slowly and your landing will be softer! What you want to achieve is to stand on the board without it moving – don't try to be clever and rock from side to side because the board will do that for you anyway.

Much the same principles apply as to the unicycle. You need to stand up straight with a bit of give in your knees, feet about two foot part – the stance you want is the one that might rebuff someone running at you, in other words, the most solid position you could be in. Put the board on the roller with one end of the board on the floor. Put one foot on the lower end, the other higher up, so you're still "on solid ground". Find some small object that is at your head height in front of you – a detail in a picture or a light switch or a particular brick in the wall – and keep your focus on it.

Then you want to take your weight over towards the middle, and the board travels with you. Get the feel of it first before you let go. The art is to make your hips do the work. The top half of your body remains quite still and you could drink a cup of tea if you wanted to, while the hips and legs are doing all the adjustments necessary. You want to try to keep the top half of your body right above the roller, so your legs might swing to one side but you and your cup of tea stay where they are. If you feel yourself coming off, don't take one foot off because you will fly in one direction and the rola bola in the other. Try to control it. Letting the board out as far as it will go to one side will mean having all your weight firmly above the roller on one leg but the toes of your other foot will be gently resting on the other end of the board. As the board comes back in again so you transfer your weight appropriately. Once you learn to stay on and then control it, you can begin to make it look difficult by swaying from side to side and looking as though you're losing your balance. There are little tricks too that look more impressive than they are. Instead of mounting it as described, you can balance the board on the roller and then jump on – if you use a bigger roller that's the only way you could get on. You can jump and turn, so that you're facing the other way. Extra height can be gained by using blocks and more boards.

Rola bolas are popular with children because you can do all sorts of pratfalls trying to get on and stay on, and small children get deliriously happy if you keep falling over! I use a rola bola to tell the story of St Peter, or Rocky, who is always in the right place at the right time but never quite gets it right. And every time he gets it wrong, off I come. In the Christmas story I mentioned earlier, the clown goes round the back of a pub once he's arrived in Bethlehem to see if he can find anything he can busk with. He finds an old box and a pile of logs, so he rola bolas on that. The box ends up as Jesus' crib. I've used it to tell the story of the Fall with the rola bola as the forbidden plaything in the garden, with an apple on the lower end. When I jumped on the other end it went flying up in the air and I was lucky enough to catch it! You could put a simple boat shape around the board and tell the story of the stilling of the storm.

My speciality is a slackrope, which is like a tightrope except it's slack! It's my slackrope of faith because it's narrow, wobbly, dangerous, but exhilarating. Once you're on it, it's wonderful, but it's difficult to get on. Once you've been on it, life can never be the same again. It's a whole routine which works well because it's skilful clowning on improbable equipment that's appropriate to the message and understandable and enjoyable on all sorts of levels. That's what the search is for. If skills or even sermons are gratuitous, then they're not really worth doing. People need symbols and images that leave lasting visual impressions. My slackrope has people on the edge of their seats – the best place for any congregation to be. To express the Word physically is to make the Word flesh: to make the Word incarnate rather than dilute it into more words is to tell the story of Christian faith. When a clown does it in such absurd ways he talks powerfully of the absurdity of that faith and the foolishness of God.

But it must be done well. There is a tendency for Christians to think that they can either get away with being, or even that they ought to be, amateurish, and that anyway there's always the Holy Spirit who can speak and work through our most feeble efforts. What nonsense! The Holy Spirit could do a lot more if we did it a lot better. We need to pursue excellence, ''to be perfect even as our heavenly Father is perfect'', to present the Gospel as well as ourselves in the best way that we possibly can. To aspire to less than that is to do a grave injustice to the God in whose image we are made.

So if you are going to try to learn skills or be physical, be sure to look after your body. Do warm-up exercises that stretch your muscles, otherwise you might pull one before you've even started. Try to do exercises each day, along with your prayers, so that you are in tune with your body as well as your soul. Try to practise the skills till you've got them right and can present them well. Presentation is important because we come back to the principle that it's how you do it that matters. Having been to Fool Time I'm a much better performer for having learned performance techniques, and it might be appropriate for you to learn some of those at some stage because it will help you to communicate much better.

There's a chicken and egg situation about circus skills because you either learn the skills first and then see how you can use this newfound talent, or you see an opportunity for a circus skill and then learn it. I keep telling myself that I'll learn the diabolo and the devil-sticks as soon as I can think of a use and place for them, and yet I'm sure if I learned them they would be useful and I would find a place for them. "Manyana" cries the Fool, knowing he'll never do it! Fool Time offered the opportunity of learning trapeze but that didn't appeal to me at all. Trapeze is painful, it is difficult to set up in places that aren't geared to it, and it doesn't actually suit my clown. Unless there was a bizarre interpretation of the Ascension I'm not sure how I'd use it anyway. So choose skills that are appropriate to you as well as to the Gospel, learn them, and then go out to play.

8

Parables and Punchlines

LET ME TELL YOU my favourite "religious joke"! It's based on John 8 and is quite biblical. It concerns the woman caught in the act of adultery — I assume not literally caught unless she was swinging from the chandeliers! The people of the town take her outside the city walls to stone her to death, as was the custom. All of a sudden Jesus appears amongst them, goes to the woman's side, and starts drawing in the sand. After a while he looks up and says, "Let he who is without sin cast the first stone". They all start to turn away, and even St John admits that the eldest turn away first — perhaps they've had longest! Then, to the amazement of all, an old woman forces her way through the crowd with a huge boulder above her head. She crashes it down on the woman's head, killing her stone dead. Jesus looks up, absolutely livid, and shouts, "Mother, you spoil everything!"

It's my favourite joke because it's funny, first and foremost. But it also has a classic structure. It starts from the familiar, suddenly goes off on a tangent, and ends with a brilliant punchline. It also has something to say about Jesus, about Mary, and about concepts of sin. It's a good example of the use of humour to say important things. It was a method that Jesus used often. The example we have includes one of his classic punchlines, "Let he who is without sin cast the first stone". It has become part of our vocabulary and language, even if most people have no idea

131

of the context. It's always the punchline that people remember. In its time it was inevitably a showstopper. It didn't have them laughing in the aisles, it was more a punch in the solar plexus, but it did the trick.

Perhaps a lot of what we find in the gospels, the synoptic ones at least, are cherished punchlines salvaged from long-forgotten stories. That's not to say that John's gospel isn't full of humour, it's just a bit short on one-liners! Other stories remain in all the gospels, full of twists and turns and surprising denouements, and if we allow Jesus his sense of humour we too can get the jokes. Then it's the clown's job not just to retell the jokes but to recreate them, to tell them in his own foolish and peculiar ways. I don't want clowns doing drama in church because anyone can ''do drama'' in clown costumes. Clowns can do routines and that's different.

What would a clown do to find a lost coin or a lost sheep? And what would he do when he found them? How would a clown tell the story of the priest who walked by on the other side, or would he just become him and do it? How would he tell the story of the Pharisee and the publican in the temple? How would he become the man who wore the wrong clothes to the wedding feast, or be one of the foolish virgins, or call at his neighbour's in the middle of the night and ask for bread? What about the story of the boy with five barley loaves and two fishes, or the waiter at the wedding feast, or Peter's mother-in-law, or the man who clocked on first in the vineyard? If a fashion-conscious clown came in on stilts with a great list of things that he couldn't eat for lunch, would we begin to consider the lilies of the field or just conclude that today has enough troubles of its own? If a clown tried to sell you a fish on the pretext that it had swallowed enough money to cover your tax bills, would you believe him? If he threw a custard pie into your face, would you turn the other cheek? If he asked you for your coat, would you give him your shirt as well? If he told you that the trouble with Nick O'Demus was that he took things too literally, would you sympathize?

If a clown were John the Baptist he could have a wonderful time with a diet of locusts and an itchy shirt, but would the punchline be an apology for not having a sense of humour? If a clown were Legion, would he express his gratitude for being delivered but rue the fact that his dinner had just fallen over the cliff? Would the clown who never saw Christ hungry or thirsty or sick or in prison complain that he wasn't wearing his name badge, so it wasn't fair? Or would he swear blind that he hadn't seen anyone with a long white robe and golden hair since the Royal Wedding?

One non-Christian clown complained to me that I had an unfair advantage because of all the material there was that I could take straight out of the Bible. There is plenty for clowns to play with, but it is best to find it for yourselves. When you find something that tickles your sense of humour or see something that could be wonderfully absurd, then you need to translate it in your on way. You are the only one who can do it in your clown's way. If you do it because you think it's funny, other people might find it funny too. If you do something that's ''supposed to be funny'' but you're not quite sure, you can be quite sure that other people won't be too sure either!

There are all sorts of ingredients that clowns can mix into their routines. We've already looked at circus skills and mentioned the possibility of magic tricks, even duff ones.

But be slightly careful about creating confusion in people's minds over the connections between miracles and magic. If we present a trick as miraculous, what are we saying about miracles? To do the old magic trick of turning water into "wine" in church is a nonsense, and it isn't sufficient to explain that Jesus could do it properly!

Essential components of clown routines are trips and pratfalls and basic slapstick. By slapstick I don't mean custard pies, but slapstick fighting, where punches and slaps are faked, and things like walking into doors or pillars. In other words, slapstick is the art of seeming to get hurt without actually getting hurt! You can't learn that in a book because it's all to do with timing – or at least, not in this book anyway. It is the same with pratfalls. The basic principle is that you should never land on any joints of your body, like your knees or elbows, or try to break your fall with your hand. Keep your head under control too so that it doesn't flop. But it depends which way you're falling as to how you do it and we can't go into that here. Trips are worth practising. Again it is difficult to describe, but as you're walking along, you need to catch, say, your right foot on the calf of your left leg without telegraphing it by changing your rhythm. Your left leg stays rooted as if it has stuck behind the paving stone, or whatever you decide you've tripped on, which throws you and your head back a bit before the momentum of your right foot continuing its journey through takes you forward and on. Don't fall over with it, and do react – look back and see what it was you tripped on.

Puns and plays on words can keep people guessing or groaning or both! The Bed of Heaven was one of my better efforts, using a Z-bed that seemed impossible to erect, as was the Sewer who went out to sew his seat. How about a whole barber shop sequence based on the premise or promise that "Not everyone who calls on the name of the Lord shall be shaved".

Mime is always useful as long as it is simple and clear. Movement, like words, shouldn't be mumbled so that they all run into each other and become quite indistinguishable. Mime is another art that must be done with conviction – if you don't believe the box you've just put down is there, neither will anyone else. Make sure objects are given their due weight and size. If you put a huge box down, don't forget it's there and walk through it – walk into it or trip over it by all means, but don't ignore it. And please don't be too stylized unless your clown is. Mime should come naturally and help us create the scene. Scene setting and creating the atmosphere can be done beautifully, but if you want us to see a herd of Gadarene swine, we can only see it through your eyes, so you have to see them too.

Audience participation is almost compulsory! This can be the verbal variety with "Oh yes I can – Oh no you can't" or getting people to join in with magic words or count something in. If you are enjoying it, they will join in and enjoy it too. You mustn't regard it as their duty to join in, and then feel let down if they don't. If you're brave, you can get people up to do things or, braver still, have things done to them. Don't drag anyone up who doesn't want to. If somebody is desperately looking away from you and not wanting to be asked, leave him alone. The best people to choose are those you know to be "good sports" or those who you can see are enjoying you enormously, e.g. the man at the back guffawing, or the kid at the front who's full of excited suggestions. I've found vicars and bishops are usually game!

Exaggeration is another tool at your disposal. As in the circus, this can take the form of outsize props such as huge hammers or fig leaves or salt pots. It can go the other way too, so you might have a tiny Bible or Bonsai fig tree or buried treasure. You can use exaggeration for comparison, like the camel going through the eye of a needle. Taking things to their logical conclusion is another clown's device for getting himself into all sorts of trouble − ''I mustn't even look at that nice man in the front row or my eye will be gouged out, or touch the altar or the Vicar will chop my hand off . . .'' And don't be afraid to use exaggerated movement that is nice and big and understandable.

There is also a whole fund of traditional circus clown routines that can be adapted. One year at the Clowns Convention in Bognor we tried using comedy cars to do the story of the house built on rock and the house built on sand. The house built on sand was the comedy car whose doors fell off and everything either fell apart or exploded − JoJo did his usual routine. Then the decent car that was newly built and polished was supposed to come in to show us how cars ought to be built and looked after, but it wouldn't start and so never made it! The best laid plans . . .

Another routine centres around one clown wanting to play a musical instrument, usually a very noisy brass one, who is stopped by a Whiteface, who takes the instrument away from him, and tells him, ''You can't play here''. The Whiteface strides off, only for the Auguste to produce another instrument from his cavernous clothing, concede that he can't play here, but then have the brainwave that he can play over there, moving to the other side of the ring. The Whiteface returns, and so it goes on. You could change it completely so that it centres around "You can't pray here". It could have the Whiteface desperately wanting peace and quiet, so the routine ends up saying something about the Peace that only Christ can bring. It could work towards the man who must leave his gift at the altar and be reconciled with his brother first. It could end up with both playing instruments and the congregation singing. It could go in any direction!

There are standard water gags, of course. One ends with water being poured into a bucket that is "balanced" on a pole, although the water actually travels down the pole and the bucket either has confetti or strings of silver paper in it, as the audience discover to their relief when it is accidentally or intentionally spilt all over them. It might go to show that it rains on the righteous as well as the unrighteous, especially if you've got soaked already. People do like a bit of mess, especially if it's on other people!

A Tramp clown routine involves coming on in the darkness and gently sweeping up the spotlight that's left in the centre of the ring, making it smaller and smaller until it's small enough to put in a pocket. This could say something about "Nobody lights a lamp and hides it under a bushel", as the Tramp decides to throw it back up into the air so that it lights everybody up. An old routine that I do is to try and persuade a stuffed dog to jump through a hoop. My punchline is that the dog is rather a backward dog, so I sometimes call him God just to annoy him. Yet however hard I try, I can never get God to jump through the hoop. He never does what I tell him.

Next time you go to a traditional circus which has good clowns, watch what they do and see if you can adapt it. The entrées are there for all clowns to use so we as clowns ought to be using them. It's also the way of telling parables because you start with what's already there, use it, but give it a twist and a powerful punchline. It doesn't have to be a Cecil B. de Mille production with a cast of thousands. Things can be very short and extremely effective. Keep it simple and make the message clear, but without having to spell it out – jokes that have to be explained are tiresome. Even Jesus found it frustrating to have to explain everything to his disciples. If you're doing a routine or entrée, give it a good start and yourselves a good entrance, provide a good middle, and serve up a surprising end. Take your time too. Clowns can take ten minutes to tie up a bootlace never mind tell a story – don't rush to the punchline and heave a sigh of relief. And make sure you continue to engage the audience by looking at them, responding to them and involving them, rather than ignoring them and thereby shutting them out as well as up.

There are all sorts of ways of creating your own stories, retelling the parables, and finding the humour in the Bible, but let me offer a few exercises which might help. The first is setting group tableaux. A tableau is like a still photograph from a film which has captured the moment and epitomized the whole story. The leader offers a title and the idea of the exercise is that the group create images that not only express it but capture its essence, not by great discussions but by quickly and silently moving into position, each responding to their own and others' inspiration. So if I then tell the group or groups to show me springtime, they should instantly become burgeoning trees and blossoming flowers, with young lovers skipping in the spring sunshine or whatever. They shouldn't be moving, because we need the equivalent of a freeze frame. The group needs to try to work together rather than have a number of obviously different images that are only loosely connected – when you start playing, you'll notice the difference.

After Springtime and a few titles like Paris, the House of Commons, Niagara Falls, the Maths Lesson, Baby's First Bath or The Rush Hour, we then move onto biblical titles. So we might try the Garden of Eden, Noah's Ark, David and Goliath, Samson in the Temple, Abraham sacrificing Isaac, the Crossing of the Red Sea. The group can't just portray characters, they have to be the sea and the ark or whatever. Moving on to the New Testament, it might be the Birth of Jesus, Turning Water into Wine, the Last Supper, the Annunciation, Feeding the Five Thousand, the Scourging of Jesus, the Crucifixion, the Empty Tomb, the Road to Emmaus, the Ascension. You can choose any scene or moment that strikes you, but once they've all warmed sufficiently to the task, they also have to add a comic or foolish dimension. That might mean one person finding a comic angle that just sets everything off nicely, or it might mean the whole group presenting a spoof, but it should add to the story rather than just parody it. The humour should not only get the onlooker thinking but also make him look at the story in a new light.

Sixty-Second Parables are fairly frantic but educational! Divide into pairs, and tell each other a true story about yourself which typifies you in sixty seconds. It's a way of warming up and we are our own best material for stories. You also realize how long or short that time is. The next task is to tell a story of fiction in sixty seconds – one that you know of old. Try to give the story a good start and finish within the time limit. Then try improvising a story of your own within the time limit. At last we come to the parables, and the task is to tell a biblical parable in sixty seconds. The final task is to create a parable of your own with its own punchline (which could be a familiar one). Having only sixty seconds teaches us to stick to the important bits of the story instead of wandering off on tangents and waffling. It gets the brain and the imagination working. Within the sixty seconds we still need to create the atmosphere so that people can enter into the story and live it themselves. A series of chronological events or bald reporting of "the facts" doesn't engage. If you can create a good story in sixty seconds it's worth it because that's probably all the time you'll get from people if you're doing street work. And most people prefer a good joke to a shaggy dog story!

Continuing the storytelling theme, try Exaggerated Parables. Start by telling an exaggerated story. It's not just the story of the fisherman and how big a fish he's caught, you need to exaggerate the detail of the story, and also its importance or its age or whatever. Use big dramatic gestures so that we begin to express it physically. Don't let it go on too long though – two minutes is more than enough. Once you've got the idea, then try it on a biblical story and see what happens. If you retell the miracles of Jesus in this way, does it make them more or less credible? If a clown tells it this way, it may be laughable but maybe we perceive its truth and do believe him.

Not everyone is very good at telling jokes, but try and tell a biblical story in a classic joke style. So the story of the Good Samaritan might start, "Have you heard the one about the priest, the Levite and the Samaritan?" Or, "Knock, knock! Who's there? Everton. Everton who? Everton who exalts himself will be humbled; whoever humbles himself will be exalted." If that doesn't get them groaning, nothing will! Limericks are always good value too. They are easy to make up and they finish with a punchline. The Feeding of the Five Thousand might be:

> They gave him five loaves and two fishes,
> Three forks, thirteen spoons and ten dishes,
> But five thousand were fed,
> Or so it was said,
> And everyone thought it delicious!

Or perhaps,

> There was a young rich man called Jim,
> Eternal life interested him,
> But faced by the price
> Of his wealth by the Christ,
> He decided it was only a whim.

Double Acts provide you with someone to bounce off and spark with. Put two pairs together so that each pair has an audience to perform to. Get the audience pair to sit while the performers stand. The first exercise is to invent a story between the two of them that purports to be based on a common memory. So it might start, "Do you remember the time we saw that gipsy caravan in the High Street?" Then the other person has to carry on "Oh yes! With that fierce-looking old woman up on the driving seat." The other continues, "Reminded me of Margaret Thatcher, actually!" And so it goes on, each jogging the other's memory and taking the story on a bit further. It must have a storyline, however bizarre, and an obvious finish, in other words the reason for telling it in the first place. You can put in as much humour as you like! Once both pairs have had a go, try the same method on a biblical story as though both of you had been there. It offers the possibility of adding all sorts of detail, atmosphere and ludicrous sidetracks along the way.

Once you've tried it with you both agreeing on the memory and story, try it with disagreement. The art is to change a detail and then take the story off in a different direction. Your partner then changes something from your bit and carries on. We still end up with a story but without the bickering! It's something of a status game. Try a biblical story with one of you as a Whiteface and the other an Auguste. Either the Auguste keeps getting it wrong and Whiteface gets increasingly irritated at having to correct him and put him back on the rails. Or Whiteface can tell the story and Auguste keeps interrupting, either with asides or red herrings or perverse explanations.

Any size group from two upwards can try physicalizing a story. One person tells the story in words while everyone else has to articulate it physically in all its detail. Mime isn't allowed. If someone has to go through a door, someone has to be the door. If it's a stormy night, we have to see the storm. The storyteller can have a great time if he or she wants to include ever more difficult details and events, but that also gives scope for the others to clown. A shrug, a look, a threat, a token feeble attempt, or a deliberate misinterpretation works wonders if it's well timed and not overdone. The exercise can also be done with all members of the group getting a chance to be the storyteller and take the story on. If you do it that way, then the storyteller must always stand outside the action. You therefore need to find obvious moments when a new storyteller can come out of the picture and change roles without interrupting the flow of the story or the performance. The storyteller should also try and use what the group are offering. If you are doing the story of the Prodigal Son and wonderful things are happening in the pigsty, use it and take it further before returning to your story.

Clowns should always use what they're given, capturing the moment and grasping opportunities. If you make a mistake, don't collapse in a sorry heap or stand on your dignity and pretend it didn't happen. Use it, embrace it, laugh at it, see where it takes you, and then come back if and when it's appropriate. If there's an interruption from your audience, don't ignore it, it might be very funny. If somebody comes in terribly late to take their seat, the oldest gag in the world is to show him up by wagging a finger and pointing at your watch, raising your eyes to the heavens. "Must be an Anglican" might be a good one-liner if delivered right and if it's appropriate to the "victim" – he needs to enjoy the joke as well. If there's a loud crash, drop down dead or make an appropriate silly comment such as "Oh well, it saves washing them". For clowns, nothing is sacred, and that includes your carefully rehearsed script and performance! Use what you're given by others, and use what you're given by God. And be grateful!

9

Principles and Practicalities

BOTH PRINCIPLES AND PRACTICALITIES have been interwoven throughout this book but I shall try to encapsulate them here, even if it means repeating some of what has gone before. The basic principle of holy fooling, Christian clowning, clown ministry, call it what you will, is that you live up to that calling. That means doing justice to both clowning and the Gospel. You can't put on a red nose, wear a "Smile. God loves you" sticker, fall on your face, and hope that does the trick. You have to take both the Gospel and clowning seriously if you want to express one through the other.

One golden rule enshrined in most if not all clown organizations is that once you are "in slap", i.e. once you are in make-up and costume, then you must be true to your clown and the show always goes on. So there are rules that forbid smoking and drinking in public because it presents the wrong image and sets a bad example. An ancient tradition is that you should neither eat nor drink anything in slap, not because of public opinion but because of the awesome responsibility of being a clown. It testifies to that otherworldliness of the clown who is yet of this world. Be that as it may, if you have just spent twenty valiant minutes trying to entertain some children, you can't shoo them away afterwards because you're off for a pint or sit scowling in the corner having a cigarette! If at the same time you have been trying to present the Good News, however briefly or implicitly, you can't just clock off. Just as a Christian must be a Christian all of the time, so a clown must be a clown all of the time. Once you've changed and returned to anonymity, that's different – though that doesn't, of course, apply to being a Christian! The idealist in me also says that you should remain a clown all the time, whichever costume you happen to be wearing, if you wear a costume at all. My clown is a clerical clown with dog-collar on, and my clown name is the same as my ''proper'' name, mainly because it testifies to my attempt to have integrity as both clown and priest and to be the same whichever dog-collar I happen to be wearing.

Only a fool tries to be perfect, and yet the pursuit of excellence is incumbent upon us. It matters that both your make-up and your costume look good. When you start it will be all a bit rough and ready, but you need to persevere and practise and get help where necessary. With costume you can comb the jumble sales and charity shops to begin with until you find exactly what you want, but then do it properly and have it tailor-made. Much better to have an original costume than be seen in tired jumble or the same as another clown or, worse still, someone in the audience! Incidentally it also gives you the chance to have a suit with lots of cavernous pockets, and number and size of pockets are crucial. In the same way, it is much better to have individual props than to depend on things that any child can buy in a jokeshop or good toyshop. Get decent shoes or clown boots too, if you can afford them. Looking good isn't a substitute for being good, but it does grant you authority and credibility. If it looks as though you care about your appearance, people will assume you care about your clowning. The pursuit of excellence also involves going to workshops, learning from others, sharing ideas, reading and researching. Try to be the best clown in the world – in all humility, of course!

You can't be a clown in private because clowning depends and feeds on response and relationship, and the clown is only discovered in community. Our own clown is found deep in our vulnerability and we need other people to be vulnerable with. Our clown is found in performance and he needs an audience. He is found in instinct and action not in thought processes. I had to start clowning rather than just talk and preach about clowns and clowning because having clowns on the brain is the worst place for them to be. The more we perform as clowns, the more we discover about our own clown. Our clown is the performer inside us who strives to be the star of the show and yet is only allowed on stage occasionally. He's too often regarded as the gap-filler, a sometimes humorous but foolish link who tries to make connections for us, but who we find much too embarrassing. We would rather not be on stage at all but remain sitting safely in the audience, politely applauding the more respectable performances that we can muster. It is much easier to send a representative than send our real selves. But the clown, in his efforts to get in on the act, of course becomes the star of the show and he's the one the people want to see. He's the one who unearths our real self. He is what our lives and what the circus is about.

Clowns take risks. They go for it. They keep setting new limits and boundaries by breaking taboos and dismantling barriers. They enter sacred places not to desanctify or desecrate them but to explore and wonder at them, and find the door that leads to another yet more sacred place.

They try to banish fear from our lives so that we can be free of its debilitating effects. Clowning is not for the timid and timorous, although that doesn't stop a clown character being timid! But the best clowns don't go too far, they don't go 'over the top'. They get it just right – they have to encourage everyone else to follow. One small step for a clown might be a very big one for the rest of mankind! Clowns take risks and they're risky to be with too. As they keep entering vulnerable places, so we are beckoned to join them.

I was asked to be part of the clergy conference for the Canterbury Diocese and had no brief. It was to last for three days and I didn't know a soul. I knew I had to bounce around a bit and had thought I wouldn't get into slap for the first session but just get the feel of things and the people. My instinct made me reverse that decision, and a bewildered gathering of 350 clergy who had been patiently waiting for the Archbishop to address them beheld a clown dusting the stage area and the seat he was to sit in. They dutifully stood up when I motioned that they should, but then I told them to sit down again. I led the Archbishop in with my feather duster aloft like a verger's wand, dusted him down, and then let proceedings commence. A short service followed which included some rather heavy if not pretentious poetry. I quickly jotted down my own verse and recited that. It worked beautifully because it was an appropriate risk at exactly the right moment and it was what the situation and service needed and demanded. In the space of the first half hour of that conference, I had introduced several sides of myself and of clowning, and it set me up for the rest of the conference. I continued to take enormous risks and most of them came off. If I hadn't taken those first risks I'd have been sunk, and I daresay I would never have established myself or my clown at all. The art of debunking is a fine one, and yet that is often the clown's task and duty. They can set the tone and the standards and create the right atmosphere.

Yet clowns allow space for people to live in. They cramp nobody's style and intrude into no one's space. Clowns keep inviting people into their own space, and equally they wait to be invited before attempting intimacy. It's the difference between inviting yourself to tea unannounced, which clowns will always do and that's fine, but then waiting to see if a seat at table is offered rather than sitting down regardless. Clowning shouldn't be at anyone else's expense – only at your own cost. Allowing the space is a mark of the clown's playfulness and vulnerable love. You can't force people to love nor can you make them come out to play, but you can keep inviting and tempting and teasing.

Clowns are truthful. They must be true to themselves and their own foolishness, but they also speak of truth and can represent it. They know how things are and speak of how they could be. They offer a different and sometimes divine perspective. They are prophetic. They are the licensed truth-tellers, both commissioned and expected to speak of things that only they can, in ways that only they know. They know that truth cannot be told outright, it can only be conveyed. With a mixture of wisdom and humour they hope that others get the joke, and that they get it without having it explained to them.

Clowns are teachers. They teach others about themselves and their lives, not with words necessarily but by their example and their antics. The clown holds up a mirror to other people so that they can see their own foolishness. We recognize our own folly reflected in him, and in laughing at him we can at last laugh at ourselves. Clowns remind us of the joy of abundant living and the truth that lies at the heart of it. Christian clowns must be full of the Good News, presenting the Way, representing the Truth, and living the Life.

Clowns need not be happy but they must be funny! They know the value and need of laughter, its hope and its healing, and they are its agents and provocateurs. They offer the prospect and perspective of humour. But that doesn't mean we have to have a huge fund of jokes and anecdotes – it means that we should *be* funny rather than say funny things or even do funny things. The basic principle is that if you're trying desperately hard to be funny it means that you're desperate, not funny! The audience can't split their sides if you've bust a gut! There are some things that are usually guaranteed a laugh, like pratfalls for small children or a tried and trusted routine. But we still have to do it right and be funny. If you fall and they think you've hurt yourself, it backfires.

Clowns need to be funny, but not all the time. A barrage of attempted humour is exhausting for everyone. Clowns need space to be angry and sad and fearful and lonely, and to express all the other feelings and emotions to which we all are prey. And they offer space for us to do the same. Clowns are moving because of their own emotions and because of the way they enable us to get in touch with ours too. Clowns can be passionate or ferocious or romantic or nostalgic. They help create the atmosphere in which things can happen. Feelings may run riot, respectability collapse in mirth, love blossom, or gloom and sorrow descend like nightfall, and there stands the clown in the midst of the maelstrom, visibly affected and obviously changed by the experience. He can choose to be funny and laugh it all off. Or he can dare to feel it and share it before moving on with a redeeming smile, assuring us that all will be well – and in the laughter of hope and a tear in our eye we believe him. The clown's capacity for tragedy will determine his competence at comedy. Perhaps that's the difference between clowns and comics. Clowns have that tragic dimension that comedians don't. And there's a sense in which while we naturally fear for him we also fear him. A three-year-old can be scared stiff by a clown, and we never quite lose that original fear. We may fear him for what he is and what we could be. Clowns evoke and provoke all kinds of conflicting emotions and responses. Don't just go for laughs.

Now all this might seem highflown or frightening or whatever, but it is simply a counsel of perfection from a clown who remains an idealist! This book is subtitled, ''A call to Christian clowning'' but it could equally be ''A call to Clowning'' because clowning is so important and has such mystical and mysterious connotations and connections. I would love everybody to discover the clown within them which is why it's a call to clowning. And while it is addressed to you as an individual, it is also a call to you to find a group in which you can discover that clown. If clowning is as important as I think it is, then it is worth the effort to try to persuade others to join you, to find kindred spirits foolish enough to accept the invitation to play in the clown's kingdom.

When I became vicar of St Paul's, Furzedown, I grasped

the opportunity of trying to establish a clown ministry group, but it didn't work out. We had two-hour workshops every Sunday evening in the church. I thought it was important to have them in the church because it put the clowning in context. We paid people to come and teach, and there were about eight different tutors, each specializing in slightly different fields. Workshop participants had to pay too, and we had a nucleus of people, some parish-based and others from further afield. People came and went, and in the end we stopped them because the financial burden was too great and we weren't really getting anywhere. But if I was to start again I would tackle it quite differently, and the fault at Furzedown lay at my door.

While I think it was right to get professional tutors to lead each workshop session, there wasn't the continuity that a central person could have provided. I always used to take a back seat and let people get on with it. While I continued to make all sorts of connections in my own mind, I wasn't willing nor did I really have the confidence to assume that mantle. It meant that we didn't have any real direction, and it stopped a genuine cohesion of the group. I also wanted us to be perfect clowns before we could go and do things, which was stupid because it meant that we didn't have enough opportunities either to test our own clown and our development, or again to work together as a group and achieve a group identity. Because we actually clowned very little and spent more time in church practising we lost a sense of objective and that may be why people drifted in and out. Perhaps that's a lesson for the Church too!

Now I have much more experience and the confidence

so I would take on the role of focus and tutor of the group and try to find appropriate opportunities for the clowns to go out and perform. At Furzedown I knew in the back of my mind that what we were doing wasn't quite right and yet I didn't know what the alternative was. I wasn't willing to take the risk of leading the workshops myself, and maybe the time wasn't right. But if you want to start a clown ministry group, somebody must make sure that the group attends to purpose and direction. If the people coming in to lead the group aren't achieving what you want, find someone else or simply have the courage to explore it together as a group. We never did the sort of things I described earlier, as far as I can remember, but that's the way that I have since found to the particular foolishness that I knew lay within each of us. Once the members of your group have begun to discover their own foolishness then you need to venture out. You can use regular sessions to devise material or swap anecdotes and experiences, to feed back to each other and encourage each other, but the sessions should become a back-up to the main work rather than a substitute for it.

Local churches, charities and schools are always desperate for clowns to come and brighten up their events, especially fairs and fêtes. They are good for experience because they give the opportunity to mix and mingle and to see both how people respond to you and how your clown responds to them. Mixing and mingling gives you the chance to keep moving and not be left in embarrassing positions – you can always hurry off into the distance on some daft pretext if you're getting stuck! It's good practice too for giving people space and learning to discern who wants to play and who doesn't. You might be using a running gag or walkabout prop, like a puppet animal or a silly umbrella, but you can't just depend on the prop or do the same to everyone. Different people of differing ages need different incentives to join in and have differing perceptions both of you and what you're doing. Don't think that you've got to be 'religious' or evangelize at the same time, because these are usually occasions when faith should be seen but not heard. Much better to make sure that the programme acknowledges you're a clown ministry group from whichever churches you come from and leave people to draw their own conclusions. It is also difficult in the early stages to remain in character throughout, never mind attempting to convert people! You might find people want to join your group having seen you in action and then they may become clowns and Christians, though not necessarily in that order.

Don't be frightened of asking for money for what you are doing. It's worth building up funds to buy equipment, and if you want to learn unicycling, for instance, that's expensive. The labourers are always worthy of their pay. If your churches see you in action they may be encouraged to have a jumble sale to support you or even just to donate some money to the cause. Costumes and greasepaint are expensive, and while some members may be able to afford them, others may not. At Furzedown the local borough Arts Council gave us some regular funding, and that was a great help. In return they expected some performances at elderly persons' clubs and the like, and that we were able to do. I think in my back-pedalling way I managed to reduce it to an absolute minimum, which again was very short-sighted of me because it meant we ended up with reduced funding as well as missing out on vital experience.

One of the first things you discover when you venture out as a clown is that, contrary to your fond hopes and belief, not everyone loves a clown! You are bound to get teased and jeered and sometimes mocked, and you have to learn to cope with that. I always get teased about having big feet, which is hardly wounding to my pride, but there are often jibes about a clown's appearance and costume. But it's what's inside that matters, not what you wear on the outside. You know that the costume you wear looks foolish because it's supposed to be, so if other people find it foolish it's hardly surprising! You might want your costume admired, and it will be by some people, but it won't be by everyone.

Some taunts might rankle, but if they hit home it may be that there is some truth in them. We need the grace to take some of that on board. If someone looks at you and obviously thinks you're remarkably childish to be all dressed up like that, you must be doing quite well in your pursuit of childlikeness! If another writes you off as a third-rate clown, reassure yourself that you're still a learner, that you will improve, and anyway at least he called you a clown and not something else! If there is a jibe that keeps recurring, find a rejoinder that makes light of it and raises a laugh, or maybe just shrug sadly and slope off. Insults can present opportunities for foolish responses and indeed whole clown routines if you take it to its logical extreme. If you take off your coat because someone doesn't like it, it could develop into a whole cod strip routine – or part of one, at least! In a way, once you are "in clown" there is no point in taking insults personally because most insults are aimed at clowns in general rather than at you as a particular one. The person doing the mocking knows nothing about you or your history or your reasons for clowning, and there is no reason why he should. If you can respond with an impromptu routine, he might just change his tune if not his mind about clowns. Don't take the weight of the world's insults on your shoulders 1 use them as opportunities for clowning!

If you find you get nervous beforehand, so you should! If we lose that feeling, we lose that sense of performing on the edge of the precipice which is where all clowns must be. If the stomach churns it gets everything else going too! Like walking on the tightrope, once you've started you just go for it and enjoy it. Once you're out there, just let the clown, the performer take over!

As a clown ministry group you will want to do things in church so you need to persuade the local vicar or minister to let you loose on his congregation. Hopefully your own congregation will welcome your contribution and insights, but a prophet isn't always honoured in his own country. The most likely opportunity is something like a Family Service. Don't feel you've got to present routines or sketches straightaway – you may not have the confidence to do that. Perhaps begin by offering to welcome people at the door, give them their books and chaperon them to their seats – dusting the seats in the process and their occupants if they want to be. Then next time you might be involved in taking the collection and doing something at the offertory, so that you become part of the service. Perhaps the next time you feel confident enough to offer a routine or sketch as part of the service that says something about the theme of the day. Finally you reach the stage where you can offer material that interprets all the readings of the day. By taking it gradually it allows the congregation to begin to appreciate you and it allows you to get the feel of performing and clowning in church and to assess what that particular congregation might respond to. When it comes to doing special services or when you are well established, then you get the chance to present ways of worship as well as interpretations of scripture.

It is valuable if you can do some teaching about it beforehand, partly to warn people but also to help them tune into the right wavelength. Somebody might preach about the traditions of holy folly or the foolishness of God or the humour of the Bible. You might be able to put an article in the parish magazine or the weekly newsletter about the group and its aims. You could try to visit some of the church groups beforehand, either to perform or to talk about what you're doing. It might ensure some support as well as understanding. You might get new members too. But do explain, don't apologize – never apologize for presenting the Gospel or for clowning.

Not all your group will want to specialize in performances in church, so try to find opportunities for ministry in the community. If there's a hospital near you you might be able to go and visit. You and they may be happy for you to try it as a one-off visit, but many hospitals would prefer an ongoing commitment. A group can take this on more easily than an individual, both in terms of availability and covering absence as well as the mutual support that such work benefits from so much. In hospital visiting don't charge in, make lots of noise and generally be a confounded nuisance. It's partly mix and mingle clowning, taking each person on his merits and weighing up their condition as well as circumstances. You don't tickle the foot of a broken leg! But it's also a chance to exercise a ministry of touch, to gently and quietly hold hands, to touch the untouchable and untouched, to kiss foreheads and backs of hands. The ministry of touch affirms people as individuals who are loved rather than patients who are treated. A clown can bring hope and healing into people's lives. Patients who haven't smiled in months may chuckle like mad, and people who haven't communicated with a soul will suddenly become chatter-boxes, as the clown breaks down the barriers with his vulnerability and love. There's no threat or status or kudos or polite but patronizing concern, just a clown who has compassion, takes the time that nobody else will, and isn't afraid of physical contact without the aid of clinical gloves.

The presence of a clown in a hospice, at a deathbed, holding the hand of the dying, or gently wandering round the wards, may be a sign of hope and even a harbinger of resurrection, an affirmation of their own lives as well as the eternal life. You never quite know how you can help or have helped people, but that is the nature of ministry of any kind because it lives in the world of imponderables where nothing can truly be measured.

If you are allowed in a hospital you will probably be offered the children's ward and that's fine. But do try other wards too because that's where your best work can be done. It needs saying time and time again that clowning isn't only for children – far from it.

Having said that, another opportunity that you might pursue as your confidence increases is doing school assemblies. Most schools are only too happy to have help, especially from outside agencies and different members of the community. As long as you're sensitive to the multi-faith and multi-cultural dimensions of most schools you will be welcome. If you are funny and still get a message across, you might even be invited back as a regular! But keep it simple and fun.

Being a clown isn't easy, nor is becoming one, and nor is setting up or even being part of a clown ministry group. But nobody ever said it was! To be vulnerable and loving and funny all at the same time is a tall order for a little clown! It is, however, infinitely rewarding, an enormous privilege, great fun, and worth all the effort and practise and discipline and insults and failures and everything else. There's something about the clown that makes things happen and speaks to people in all sorts of different and sometimes extremely profound ways, and to be a part of that tradition is an extraordinary experience. While I would encourage any and every clown and would-be clown to master circus skills, learn dramatic techniques, watch and learn from other clowns, and do anything that will improve and develop their own character and ability, in the end it is a search for authenticity and the embrace of absurdity. As long as clowns continue to attempt both all will be well, whatever their level of technical ability. Your major resource, on which all will depend, is simply yourself and what is inside you.

10

Aims and Objectives

THAT EIGHT-YEAR-OLD BOY sitting in a caravan all those years ago had been seduced by the possibility of running away to the circus, to a life of adventure and bright lights. He knew it was a hard and sometimes tragic life, but it was a small and supportive community in which he could feel at home. The ups and downs, the storms and sunshine, the beautiful days and balmy nights all blended and blurred into the perfect life in which the clown would be much loved and most necessary. In the circus ring, whatever anyone said to the contrary, it was the clown the people came to see, and it was the clown who made the difference. I guess that eight-year-old boy who grew up and forgot about the circus was then seduced by the possibility of running away to the Church, which he thought might be an adventure and in which he knew he could install bright lights! It would be a hard and sometimes tragic life, but it was a small and supportive community in which he would feel at home. All the ups and downs, the laughter and tears, would blend and blur into the perfect life in which the priest would be much loved and most necessary. In church, whatever anyone else said to the contrary, it was the priest the people came to see, the vicar who made the difference.

It would be facile to conclude that I found one in the other, or even that a conflation of the two fulfilled my secret desires and ambitions. Yet it is hard to resist the conclusion that being a clown in the circus is very akin to being a priest or minister in the Church. For me they are synonymous and if I tried to separate or split the two I guess I would end up a schizoid character. I believe that I am called by God to be both clown and priest, to be his holy fool. Whether I am taking a funeral in surplice and stole, or performing in church in clown costume and big boots, I remain Roly and retain my dog-collar as a sign of it. So my premier aim and objective is to respond and live up to my calling. If asked why I do it, the answer lies in my understanding of my vocation.

If that sounds a very personal aim and objective, well maybe it is! Yet the aim and objective of clown ministry is also to encourage others to follow suit, to take risks, to be vulnerable, to love, laugh and cry. Clown ministry speaks of the God of Tears and Foolishness, of Love and Laughter, and that can be a huge challenge to some people. A major aim must be to represent that God in word and deed to all people so that all may understand, all may ultimately get the joke, and the Church that defiantly sings that it will not be moved finds that it is constantly and deeply moved. A Church that proclaimed the vulnerable lover in deed and word would be a Church that was truly spreading and living up to the Good News of the Gospel. Rather than indulging in tortuous apologetics and tying itself in theological knots, the Church could embrace the inherent absurdity of faith, acknowledge the ridiculousness of its position and predicament, and enjoy playing with its status rather than clinging desperately to it. Oh for a Church with a shrug and a mischievous redeeming smile, a tear in its eye and a heart that is broken!

The established Church in England, in all its faded dignity and tattered glory, remains prone to the dangers and temptations of impregnability and preposterous pomposity. One aim of clown ministry must be to offer the Church an image of itself, in its foolish mirror, of the only garb it has left, which is the ill-fitting livery of beggardom, the clown's motley. Perhaps then the Church could don those glad rags and tatters with glee and storm back into the world's arena to help mankind laugh at the picture of its own perversity. If the Church were prepared to fall flat on its face and have a few custard pies thrown at it, it could then start throwing a few back too!

To change the image of "the Church" means to change the outlook of the people who make up the Church, and to change some of what goes on inside our churches too. All worship, of whatever brand of churchmanship, has its own forms and rituals, and clown ministry not only offers an understanding of prayer as playful but also ritual as sacred play. If ritual is seen as play we can begin to enjoy and appreciate the rules of the game and join in too. There cannot be an inflexible, magical, proper way of doing things, that has to be followed to the letter, every last jot and tittle, for fear of the spell being broken, because that spoils the fun and loses play's perspective. If there are muddles and mistakes in worship, let's laugh if they are amusing. When I saw the banner bearer, who until then had been processing with great dignity down the aisle, get caught in the Christmas lights and trail them behind him, of course it was funny and I laughed – and I daresay God laughed too!

Ritual can become a hindrance rather than a help to worship. When the altar is shielded by a regiment of pimply youths and pompous know-alls, swathed in lace and heading for arthritic knee joints, fighting over who's going to be the thurifer this week, you begin to wonder! If the service can't go on because the incense has run out or the amplifying equipment for the music group hasn't appeared or the candles aren't lit or the vicar's still speaking in tongues in the vestry, you start to vote with your feet. Moribund and meaningless rituals that are persevered with because "that is the way it has always been done" are surely an insult to all concerned, God included, as are the party tricks and parlour games that signal a particular stance and style of churchmanship.

The clown wants to bring liturgy alive, to bring the people to the edge of their seats, to foster the imagination and creativity of all present, to allow people to worship with their souls and bodies rather than just their lips. Worship should move and teach and entertain. Let there be light and colour and laughter and tears! In worship the clown wants us to be surprised by joy, taken unawares by the Holy Spirit. We need the structures to act as the rules, shape and boundaries of the game, but there is a need for spontaneity too. Tired hymn sandwiches that have been left too long on the plate, dreary documentaries that tell us all what we're supposed to be doing, and eucharistic dramas that are merely low season repeats, don't fit the bill. Castrated liturgy cannot produce new life in the Church, has no real knowledge of or connection with renewal, and leaves us merely going through the motions.

The clown demands that we do things properly, and that we do them with a certain style, flair and panache. The slapstick man is neither slapdash nor slap-happy in that department. Worship needs a sense of theatre to allow people to enter into the drama and story that is being told and enacted. The clown would like people to come to church because they want to play, they want to enjoy and fulfil themselves, not out of reluctant or stiff-lipped duty. There needs to be a commitment to what's going on if things are going to happen. Much rather a captivated congregation than a captive audience! Worship needs a sense of humour to grant it the divine perspective, and it needs laughter to lift us out of our dull worlds into the domain of the transcendent.

Just because clowns are around doesn't mean everything has got to be crash, bang, wallop, and a laugh-a-minute momentum. Worship needs stillness too, offering a time to reflect and to treasure the moment. It's a matter not just of taking time but also of timing – silence shouldn't only be when the rubrics suggest it! Silence and stillness are times of searching, contemplation, contentedness. They allow us to do an inverted Caesar as we come, we see, and we are conquered. We need silence for our souls' sake but also, at a more mundane level, for sheer contrast and even respite. Clowns are collectors of moments, and they can change their mood and focus in an instant. One moment the clown is charging round the ring, and then suddenly he has stopped and is staring in rapt wonder at something we can hardly imagine and certainly never noticed.

A clown can offer an awful lot in a service. He may represent anarchy amidst the order, a sense of unpredictability and unimaginable possibilities, profound insights into ways of worship and meaning of scripture, and that indefinable aura of mystery that persuades us of his divine rapport. Clown ministry attempts to leave a legacy of foolishness in its wake so that others in each place will take up the mantle and even the motley to continue the work. My eight-year-old's wish for bright lights and the curate's desire to install them point to the Church being not only the Light of the World but a beacon of playfulness lit by the flames of folly.

A consequent aim and objective would be that churches become places of play for all people. That means taking the risk of opening the doors and leaving the buildings, as well as the people, vulnerable. There are many who would value the opportunity to come and sit and muse awhile, to rest and be refreshed and invigorated. A church building provides that resting place away from work and busyness, a chance to catch up on yourself and on God, a place to take your leisure.

But churches could also be places where children and adults come to play. Saturday morning theatre for children, with lots of clowns, of course. Music hall, mime, theatre, classical music, gospel music, jazz – all the performing arts should find a home in our churches. Exhibitions of art, sculpture and photography – there are all sorts of opportunities to parade the artistic skills and creativity of others, and in so doing to foster them in other people. Churches could become places where imagination can run riot and have expression. Clown ministry invites everyone to come and enjoy themselves, to have vision and visions, to dream dreams and maybe fulfil them. And why not have clowns at the door – the outsiders who welcome the outsiders in, the joybringers and dreammakers beckoning us to a world full of mystery and adventure?

There is no limit to what could be done in church buildings if we only dare. Before the days of church halls and the like, the sanctuary was set apart but the rest of the building, especially the nave, was available for everyone to use. Pews weren't screwed to the ground in those days. There would have been feasting and dancing and all manner of events that maybe today we would frown upon for having "in church". Yet in my last parish the church was used for the Christmas Fair, as a polling station in the General Election, as a concert hall, for dancing classes for the local school, for art exhibitions, and all sorts of meetings. We even used it as a temporary nursery school if and when work had to be done on the church hall. We would have had to have used incense on the Sundays in between just to get rid of the smell of nappies! Thousands entered that church who would never otherwise have dreamt of doing so, and there stands the clown teasing them that he knew he'd get them in there somehow. But for the clown nothing and everything is sacred, and every moment presents its opportunities for the Gospel and for God. Open the doors and see what happens! The church shouldn't be a place that you don't do things in, it should be the opposite – a place where you can try all sorts of things and every licence and opportunity is given, where all people really are welcome, and not just on the church's terms.

All are welcome and encouraged to be themselves, express themselves, enjoy themselves, and be true to themselves. Clown ministry encourages and pursues truthfulness. Not only do clowns try to embody truth and be the truth-tellers, the Gospel jesters, they know that they have to be true to themselves to be able to do that. You can't live a lie or inhabit a world of deceit and be truthful, full of truth, at the same time. How can anyone persuade another person of the Truth when there is no evidence of any truth in them? – enter the Pharisees and hypocrites stage left! A church is a place where you can be alone with the God from whom no secrets are hidden, where forgiveness is freely and foolishly offered, where we know we are loved for who, not what, we are, and where we begin to discover who God created us to be. Clown ministry acknowledges our imperfections, is undeterred by our failures and the times and places we fall short, debunks our pretensions, and sends us out in pursuit of Truth and our own truth once more.

Clown ministry seeks and speaks of the truth but never sells it because it is there for the taking, there to be shared. The way that some would-be evangelizers go on, it's a hard-sell marketplace where Truth is a cut-price bargain, ''sold to the lady on my right'' if she bids more than anyone else, beautifully gift-wrapped, and taken home along with numerous other little incentives and a money-back guarantee. Come back the encyclopaedia salesman – all is forgiven! The aim of clown ministry is to reawaken our sense of humour so that we can not only get the joke but share it too, conveying the truth and allowing others to own it for themselves. A sense of humour perceives the incongruous and the absurd, allows a glorious sense of perspective, establishes priorities, and measures authenticity.

One objective of clown ministry is for the clown to be the Church's prophet, priest and king. His is the prophetic, foolish voice that calls out in the wilderness. The world will have none of it, of course, closing its ears to his entreaties and branding him a fool for all his endeavours. But Jeremiah was neither the first nor the last to be given the treatment for pointing to the truth, daring to speak of and share his vision, and articulating the demands of God. As priest the clown fulfils his time-honoured role as the mediator between man and God, the messenger and go-between who somehow has the ear of God. His is the transforming sacramental touch. Encouraging and enabling, leading and inspiring, teasing and serving, he becomes the focus of the Christian community, the first and last. He is first and last, because he is both clown and king interchangeably.

It is the topsy-turvy world of God's Kingdom, and the clown reflects that. Those who revel in riding high horses should look to the example of the King who rode a donkey. Those who love to lord it over others should ponder the example of the master who washed his servants' feet. Those who make sure that their word is final might remember that the Holy Spirit might be around, trying to get a word in edgeways. The clown is a good model of ministry, not least because both clown and minister find themselves in the same boat with a similar role and function.

Both are somehow set apart from the world. However much they are at the heart of things they yet never quite belong, and remain on the fringes, looking on. Such a position allows them the role of the detached observer of society, and that vantage point offers a perspective to which few others have access. Both are marked out by their costumes, which make them easily identifiable and thus accessible – anonymous clowns or clergy in mufti seem to defeat the purpose in some ways! Both clown and priest are to be in the world and yet not of it, and both thus represent infinite possibilities in their embodiment of the promise and vision that inhabiting both worlds allows. Both have to hold the two worlds in creative tension, keeping open the channels of transcendence while being firmly grounded in this world and its affairs.

What many clergy and ministers are beginning to discover is that they fulfil the role traditionally confined to the Fool alone of "he who gets slapped". As his position in society as a whole and the local community in particular becomes less and less exalted, so the vicar of a parish finds himself the fall guy in any number of situations and in many people's eyes. No longer important by divine or any other sort of right, he faces a growing amount of mockery and abuse. Masochistic martyrdom is not the answer, nor is the dubious comfort of hiding away amongst the lives of the converted. The clown just picks himself up, dusts himself down, and keeps coming back, irrepressible as ever. As I know to my cost, some of the biggest laughs are those that produce the biggest bruises, and there are obvious connections between the two. But laughter of scorn can turn to laughter of acceptance, and often does – it is one sign of the hope that laughter offers. Getting slapped is part and parcel of ministry and we just have to turn the other cheek and get on with it.

The aim of clown ministry is to live passionately, intuitively and truthfully, so that we are in touch with our emotions, in tune with our instincts, and true to ourselves. Instant clowns who plonk on a red nose and hope for the best are on a par with plastic clergy who force a grin and hope for the best. The one person in the world I try to avoid is the clergyman rooted at the church door with glazed expression, doing a passable imitation of one of those nodding dogs in the back of a car as he mechanically shakes hands with everyone as they leave church! Cardboard cut-outs get us nowhere. Clown ministry must have sufficient spontaneity and insight to respond to the opportunity of the moment. It must also take the time to respond to each individual rather than take them en bloc. That way we ensure that we answer real needs rather than cater for the imagined ones. Clowns would rather fill our churches with slapstick saints than plastercast statues.

Clown ministry aims to speak to all ages at the same time. There will be differing levels of response and understanding but it is possible to communicate with everyone if we are visual and physical as well as verbal, and if we keep it simple. All-age worship in church finds a new dimension when the clown is around, for all the children of God are invited out to play. All-age worship isn't about reducing everything to the lowest level, the lowest common denominator. That ends up as hopelessly patronizing and neither helps nor inspires anybody. All-age worship should be what it says and allow all ages to worship in their appropriate and particular ways. The stimulus may be the same but the response will differ. Worship is a creative response to the love of God, and clown ministry seeks to articulate it.

Clown ministry would like to be rid of all those "ists" and "isms" that defeat and divide people. They categorize and restrict the people who belong, and ostracize and condemn those who don't. "Ists" and "isms" are a classic example of the place of wailing and gnashing of teeth! "Ists" and "isms" have to be taken seriously, or they would at least prefer to be. We're back to the problem of the importance of being earnest. Clown ministry desperately hopes that it will never become an "ism" otherwise clowns will become "ists". Clown ministry wants people to be strong enough to be individuals, humble enough to be human, and loving enough to care. But it is care for every person not for a type of person, care for individual people in a given situation not care for a cause. When I was a student I had a Snoopy poster on my wall that read "I love mankind. It's people I can't stand". Clowns aren't abstract or distant, they are intimate and real. Clown ministry is care and compassion with a smile and a tear and a gentle touch. Soap-boxes are for stumbling over not for standing on. Of course clowns must challenge injustice, but in their own foolish ways. It is the jester's art and calling to do so.

The call to Christian clowning is the call to be vulnerable lovers and courageous truth-tellers. All that has been said in this chapter about ministers and clergy is applicable to all Christians, for we must all minister to each other and be truthful to and for each other. It is a call to the ministry of tears in the name of the God of Tears. The call to Christian clowning is the challenge to represent in yourself the comedy and tragedy of death and resurrection, and to make its truth and import both accessible and real. Fools rush in because there is no time like the present, but they never rush blindly. Living on the edge of the precipice demands an accurate weighing of the risks, consummate balance, and a proper playfulness. Clowns may be sacrificial but they're not stupid! Where there are places that angels fear to tread, the clown steps up as the eternal volunteer, saying "Here am I, send me", for nothing is too fearful or too sacred or too much for him. Clowns are both fools and angels, messengers of God entrusted with the Good News of his Kingdom as well as the care of his children. The foolishness of God is a wonderful thing! He's just waiting for everyone to get the joke, so that both heaven and earth can resound with laughter, even the laughter of God.